Dr. T. B. Maston taught Christian Ethics at Southwestern Baptist Theological Seminary for 40 years before his retirement in 1963. He has his Ph.D. in Christian Ethics from Yale University. *The Conscience of a Christian* reflects his life-long interest and concern in relating the Christian faith to the life of the average person. His other concern—to deal in a scholarly way with ethics and ethical problems—is amply demonstrated by his two previous books published by Word: *The Christian, the Church, and Contemporary Problems;* and *Biblical Ethics. The Conscience of a Christian* is Dr. Maston's 14th book.

# THE
# CONSCIENCE
## OF A
# CHRISTIAN

# THE
# CONSCIENCE
## OF A
# CHRISTIAN

### T. B. MASTON

*Illustrated by*

### DOUGLAS DILLARD

**WORD BOOKS, Publisher. Waco. Texas**

40318

# *Preface*

The chapters of this book represent a continuing conviction that the Christian religion is concerned about and applicable to the total life of the individual and the world in which he lives. The Christian should think and pray through to defensible Christian positions regarding all the problems and issues he faces.

The problems discussed in these chapters are of three general types: individual, church and denominational, and social. An effort has been made not to evade any problem because of its delicacy or because of differences of opinion concerning it. You will discover, however, that some major problems have not been discussed. This has been due to two things. Some of them could not be discussed helpfully in the limited space we had (500-600 words). Also, there were some problems that I did not feel adequately prepared to treat.

These brief chapters or essays originally appeared in a series of one hundred and four articles for denominational papers. They were written under the general caption "Problems of the Christian Life," and were beamed to pastors but primarily to men and women in the pew. The desire to reach as many as possible through the largest possible number of publications explains their brevity and their style in general. For this volume the articles have been topically arranged; otherwise, there have been only minor corrections and changes.

Some of you may disagree with some positions taken and statements made. This will not particularly bother me. I do hope you will understand what I have said. I also hope you will think for yourself. I will say to you as I have said to students through the years: I would rather that you think and disagree than agree and not think.

Appreciation is expressed to the editors who so generously used the original articles. A special word of appreciation is due Dr.

W. C. Fields and the Baptist Press for the wide distribution given to the articles. Thanks are also due the secretaries who have been helpful in many ways, particularly Mrs. Russell Wilson and Mrs. Melvin Bridgford. The latter prepared the final typescript.

# Contents

7

# ● I.
# BASIC CONCEPTS

# 1. The Gospel:
## Individual and/or Social

THERE HAS BEEN considerable debate through the years concerning the nature of the gospel. This debate has been revived to some degree and in some circles in the contemporary period.

Some insist that Christians should be concerned exclusively with winning individuals to Christ and maturing them for Christ. They contend that we should not get involved in social issues.

It is doubtful if many people would say that Christians should be exclusively interested in social conditions and problems. Many do believe, however, that Christians should be concerned with both the individual and the world in which he lives. After all, the individual Christian does not live in a vacuum or in isolation. He lives necessarily in a particular cultural situation and in relationship to other people.

As a citizen of the world, the Christian fulfills numerous and sometimes complex if not conflicting roles. Whatever these roles may be, he cannot escape the fact that he is a Christian. The word "Christian" should precede and define every role he plays.

For example, he may be a husband and a father, but he is a "Christian" husband, a "Christian" father; and the prefix "Christian" should make a difference. So it is with every role he plays. He may be a doctor or a lawyer, farmer or banker, employer or employee, teacher or pupil, legislator or judge. He may be a member of the Chamber of Commerce or of a labor union, a white man or a Negro, a citizen of the U.S.A. or of the U.S.S.R. If he is a Christian, his faith should find a way to express itself in every area of his life.

This means that whether we like it or not, the gospel we preach and teach inevitably must be applied to every aspect of our social situation. This has to be true if we are to meet the needs of individuals, if we are concerned about the way they express their Christian faith.

The church's concern for the world will be expressed primarily

11

through the lives of redeemed men and women. There is no sound hope for a better world without better men and women, and the only hope for better individuals is to bring men and women into a vital, life-changing union with the resurrected Christ.

Redeemed men and women need, however, to know how they can effectively apply their Christian faith to the different areas of their lives. This means that churches, under the leadership of the Holy Spirit, should provide opportunities for the study of strategies and methods that can be used to influence the world and its structures for Christ and his cause.

Churches should also be concerned with conditions in society because of the effect of those conditions on men and women, boys and girls. Conditions in the home and in the community in general may make it relatively easy or difficult to reach the individual for Christ. Environmental factors will very definitely affect his spiritual growth and maturity. This suggests again that even if we were exclusively concerned with the individual, we would have to be concerned with the world in which he lives.

The gospel we preach and teach is not "an individual gospel" or "a social gospel." It is a gospel that knows no limits in its application to life. It is a message for the total man, and hence it is also a message for every aspect of the world in which we live.

# 2. The Sovereignty of God and Social Concern

CHRISTIANS today are expressing more concern for people and for social conditions in general than they have in the past. This is encouraging.

Is there a sound basis for such concern? There are several bases, but they are all ultimately grounded in the nature of God. Through our union with Christ we have been brought into the family of God. He expects us to be like him—like him in character and in concern.

This means that the limits of our concern should be determined by the limits of his concern. As the sovereign God of the universe, he was and is interested in the totality of life. He is concerned about what we do on Sunday in the house that has been dedicated to his worship and service. But, he is also concerned about what we are and what we do on Monday through Saturday in our home and neighborhood, where we work and play, on the streets—everywhere.

He is also concerned, and we too should be concerned, about every aspect of the lives of those we touch from day to day. We should remember that he knows no color or cultural limits. God is concerned for the total life of *all* people. We, the children of God, should be impartial in our concern for the total life of all men.

Because the God revealed in the Scriptures was impartial, he showed a special concern for the neglected and underprivileged. His prophets in the Old Testament were defenders of the poor, the widows, the orphans, and the strangers. We believe that God continues to have a special interest in the neglected, and that the same thing will be true of his prophets in every age.

Jesus, who revealed fully the Father, reached out in a particular way to those who suffered, to the handicapped and the moral and social outcasts of his day. If we walk in his way, we will reach out in compassion and concern to all kinds of people and particularly

13

to those in the neglected segments of our society.

The sovereign God is not only interested in the totality of the life of the individual, he is also concerned about every phase of the life of the world. God who is the same yesterday, today, and forevermore is seeking to work out his will and purpose among all peoples in every part of the world. This is the basis for our concern as individual Christians, as churches, and as denominations in the affairs of our nation and other nations of the world.

It is the sovereignty of God that sets the proper limits of our concern. It also provides the most effective motive or dynamic for social action and concern.

We also believe that the sovereign God's purposes for the world will ultimately be achieved. If we are cooperating with him in his work in the world, we can rest assured that there will come a time of ultimate victory when the kingdoms of this world will become the kingdom of our Lord and of his Christ (Rev. 11:15).

# 3. Where the Action Is

"THE BUSINESS world is where the action is." This statement was made by the president of a Chamber of Commerce to a group of college students. He was encouraging them to choose business as a career.

In recent years several bright young ministers have resigned their pastorates to enter some type of government service. Some of them have justified their action by saying, "I want to be where the action is." The implication is that the ministry and the church are not where the action is.

What is meant by the expression "where the action is"? Most who use it probably mean the place or area where something important and significant is happening. Those who have a service motive may use the expression to refer to the type of service in which they feel that they can come to grips with the real problems of people, the significant issues of our world.

Most of us would like to be where the action is. How can we know where it is? Really, can we know?

From the Christian perspective the real action is where God is at work in the world. It is the Christian's belief, however, that God is creatively active in every aspect of the life of the world. He may be unusually active in some phase at a particular point in time. Who would claim to be wise enough, however, to know where that place is?

A young minister recently asked some pertinent questions about "where the action is." "How can we know where the really significant action is? Can any man know where God is at work in some unusual way?"

He further asked, "Would any one have thought when Jesus was born that the real action was not in Caesar's household but in a manger at an inn in the village of Bethlehem?"

So it has been through the centuries. The real action, the place

where God was unusually active in the life of the world, has frequently been in some quiet spot, in some event little known by any except those immediately involved, and God himself.

This means that we should be careful about comparing the importance of places or types of service. The place where the action is for me may be quite different from the place where the action is for you. Each in his own way and in his own place is to work for and with God. And if we are where he wants us, that is where the action is for us.

Some may have a sense of divine mission while serving as a businessman, a farmer, a professional man, or in some phase of the political life of the community, state, or nation. Still others may feel that where the action is for them is as a housewife, a schoolteacher, or in a church-related vocation at home or overseas.

Each child of God should have a deepening conviction that what he is doing and where he is doing it is within the will of God. He can be sure, if he is permitting God to work out his will in him and through him, that he is, in the deepest and truest sense, where the action is.

No one of us should ever belittle the service of another. Ours may be a place of prestige and power. His may be in some isolated spot unknown to any except the Lord. He may be, however, in a place where God in some unusual way and to an unusual degree is working out his purposes for the world.

# 4. "He Went About Doing Good"

THIS FIVE-WORD biography of Jesus, "He went about doing good," was part of Peter's sermon in the house of Cornelius. The statement has deep and significant meaning for the followers of Christ.

Hoke Smith, Area Representative of the Foreign Mission Board of the Southern Baptist Convention for Spanish-speaking South America, recently said that the essence of missionary theory and practice could be reduced to a very concise formula: "To be like Jesus in attitudes, words, and deeds." This is not only the essence of missionary theory and practice, it is the essence of the Christian life. Christ's followers are to be like him.

If we are like him, we will have a wayside ministry. By that I mean that Jesus went about from place to place, and as he went he was helpful in his relation to suffering, sinning, seeking men and women. He did not settle down in one spot and invite the people to come to him. He went out where they were. Our contemporary institutionalized conception of Christian work tends to localize and circumscribe our ministry for him. We must move out of our church buildings and reach people where they are, or we will not even touch the vast majority of them.

This does not mean that there will be no need for our buildings. We will still need them for worship and fellowship. But that worship and fellowship should be primarily preparatory. Also, we should seek to discover new approaches and techniques to transport some of that fellowship out where the people are.

Let us never forget that as Jesus went from place to place he ministered to the needs of the people.

What was the secret to the kind of life Jesus lived? Peter says that he went about doing good, "for God was with him." Here was the source of his power. It was also the reason or the motive for the kind of life he lived.

At least his life was a natural expression of an inner desire. For

example, he could have used his miraculous power to have performed even more spectacular miracles than most of those he performed. They would have been signs or proofs to the people that he was the Messiah, that he was the Son of God.

Why did he use his power so exclusively to relieve human needs? Approximately two-thirds of his recorded miracles were healing miracles. All others, with the possible exception of one or two, were miracles to relieve some human need. Why? I believe that he used his miraculous power to relieve human needs simply because he wanted to. He had a deep concern for people.

The more vital our relation is to Jesus Christ, the deeper will be our desire to go about doing good. Also, the only source of the power that will enable us to have an effective wayside ministry is the power that comes from a vital relationship to him.

# 5. Christian Concern

CHRISTIANITY is a religion with a tender heart. The centrality of love is one of its most distinctive qualities. The epitome of its gospel is: "For God so loved the world . . . ." Its chief commandment is supreme love for God, and a second like it is love for neighbor. The natural expression of the Christian's love for others is his concern for them.

The real source of the Christian's compassion and concern is his vital life-changing union with the compassionate Christ. As was true of Christ, the Christian's concern will be individualized as well as generalized. For example, he will be concerned not simply for the colored peoples of the world but also for the colored individuals he knows. His heart will go out not only to the poor, the needy, the neglected in general, but also in a very special and personal way to those particular people whom he contacts from day to day.

How much have we let the compassion and concern of Christ grip our souls and express itself through our lives?

Another searching question is: How broad is our concern? E. Stanley Jones once said that he could wish that his arms were long enough to reach around every man in the world. Our love and concern should be as broad as the world and as deep as human need.

There is something wrong with us as children of God if we can look out on our world with its suffering, its sorrow, and its sin without feeling a tug on our hearts. There is something wrong if we do not have a sincere desire to do something to relieve the burdens of the world and also to correct conditions that contribute to those burdens.

Many of the people among the teeming multitudes of the world are hungry. Frank Laubach, who possibly knew the restless masses better than anybody else, said that four-fifths of them go to bed hungry every night. Among these are countless children, many of whom starve to death every year.

We need the eyes to see and the heart to feel for these starving masses who incidentally are on the move today and may remake our world tomorrow.

The Christian's concern should also be broad enough to include the old, the lonely, the insecure, and the frustrated. His heart should reach out to those who are deformed and twisted in body and who are demented and handicapped in mind.

He should be concerned about and do what he can to lift and encourage the social and moral outcasts of our society. Some of these may be among the world's untouchables, but Christ knew no untouchables. We, his followers, should not consider anyone untouchable.

The concern of Christ led to action. He had compassion; he wept. He had compassion; he healed. He had compassion; he raised from the dead. The proof of our concern is what it leads us to do.

We should do what we can for the victims of modern society. We should not restrict ourselves, however, to a healing ministry. Our concern should lead us to do what we can to correct the conditions that produce the wrecks of society.

We should not be satisfied merely to provide an ambulance at the foot of the precipice; we should build a fence and set up warning signals at the top of the precipice.

# 6. Love for God and Man

THERE IS abundant evidence in the Scriptures and in Christian experience that love for God and love for our fellowman belong together.

This is seen with particular clarity in the reply of Jesus to the lawyer who asked him what was the chief or greatest commandment in the Law. The reply of Jesus was, " 'You must love the Lord your God with all your heart, and with all your soul, and with all your mind' " (see Deut. 6:5). He then added, "This is the greatest and the most important commandment."

Jesus, the matchless teacher, possibly paused for emphasis, and then quoted again from the Old Testament (Lev. 19:18): "The second most important commandment is like it: 'You must love your neighbor as yourself' " (Matt. 22:36-39). The second is like the first in what way? Possibly like it because it was also a commandment of love. But Jesus may have meant that it was like it in importance.

The lawyer had asked Jesus for the first, chief, or greatest of the commandments. Why did Jesus also give him "the second most important commandment"? There is no way to know for sure. It may have been that Jesus knew that the lawyer and the Pharisees whom he represented needed in a particular way the second commandment. Or, it may have been that Jesus considered the two so nearly equal in importance that both were required for a satisfactory answer to the lawyer's question.

It is also possible that Jesus considered the two so closely interrelated that one was incomplete without the other.

The source of our love for our neighbor is God who is love or *agapē* (1 John 4:8, 16). In the deepest sense, love or *agapē* is the spontaneous fruit of a vital relationship to the One who is love. And we should add that the more vital and dynamic that relationship is the more love of our fellowman will characterize our lives.

Furthermore, love of God and love of neighbor are so closely interrelated that the latter is the proof of the former. John plainly says that if anyone says he loves God and hates his brother, "he is a liar" (1 John 4:20).

At the close of Jesus' reply to the lawyer, or perhaps as a part of that reply, we find the following statement: "The whole Law of Moses and the teachings of the prophets depend on these two commandments" (Matt. 22:40). Love for God and man sums up or fulfills all that is found in the Law and the prophets.

For example, the basic moral law of the Old Testament is epitomized in the Ten Commandments. Those Commandments are usually divided into two groups or two tables of the law. The first table has to do with man's relation to God and the second has to do with man's relation to his fellowman. If one loved God supremely he would keep the first table of the law. If he loved his neighbor as himself he would keep the second table.

Paul pointedly says, "For the whole Law is summed up in one commandment: 'Love your neighbor as yourself'" (Gal. 5:14). We know by what he says in Romans that he is referring to the second table of the law (see Rom. 13:8-10).

Let us summarize by saying that love for God and man belong together. Love for God, or possibly better, the love that comes from God, is the source of our love for our fellowman, and love for our neighbor or our fellowman so inevitably follows our love for God that it is proof of that love.

## 7. Love: A New Commandment

"A NEW commandment I give you: love one another" (John 13:34).

How was love "a new commandment"? Jesus had frequently spoken of love before. He had given love for God and neighbor as the summary of the Law and the prophets (Matt. 22:40). What did he mean when he called it a "new commandment"?

It may help us answer that question if we understand that there are two words that are sometimes translated "new." One means basically young as contrasted to aged; the other means fresh as opposed to worn out (see Matt. 9:17 where both words are used). In the passage from John 13 the word is "fresh."

It is possible that Jesus meant that the new commandment was new in its source. Here he was not quoting from the Old Testament as he had in the summary of the Law (Deut. 6:5; Lev. 19:18). Notice he said, "I give unto you." The authority for what he said rested within him.

The commandment was also new in motive. Our love for one another stems from his love for us. Since he has loved us, we naturally and inevitably should love one another. Through his love for us we have been brought into the family of God. We should love those within that family, those who have been brought into union with him through his love for them. The proof of our love for him is our obedience to his commandment to love one another.

The commandment he gave was and is abidingly new or fresh in its dimension. It is new in those who are to be loved. We are to love those who are in the Christian fellowship. As disciples of Christ we should love all men, but we should, in a unique way, love one another. It is similar to a man and his family. He can and should love all people, but he can and should love his wife and children in a distinctive way.

Notice also that this love was new in its expectations or demands. The disciples were to love one another as Jesus had loved

25

them. Here was both model and standard. How much had he loved them? He was going to give his life for them. They should be willing to give their lives for one another.

This quality of love for one another will be new and fresh in its consequences. It will make us friends of Christ (John 15:14). It will prove to others that we are his disciples (John 13:35).

Love for one another creates a spirit of fellowship among Christians. Love will also determine as much as any one thing the outreach of the Christian and the church to the peoples of the community and the world. The more we love one another within the Christian fellowship, the more that love will reach out beyond that fellowship to all men.

# ● II.
# THE INDIVIDUAL

# 8. God's Call:
## To All or Some?

SOME OF GOD'S calls are unquestionably to all his children. Is there in addition a unique call to some?

God's call to salvation is clearly addressed to all men. The words of Jesus, "Come, follow me," are an open invitation to all. His basic teachings apply to all who claim to know him.

What a difference it would make if those of us who sit in the pew really believed that God calls us to live on as high a moral and spiritual level as he expects of his servant in the pulpit! What a tremendous impact would be made for God on the world if every child of his believed that God expected him to have the same sense of purpose and dedication that is expected of our missionaries!

Every child of God should have a conviction that his vocation or calling is within the will of God and can be used to promote the kingdom of God. He should realize that he not only serves God and his fellowman in and through his church but also in and through his daily work.

Does this mean that there is nothing unique about a call to church-related vocations? Can we maintain a sense of call for all and at the same time believe in a unique call for some? A failure to answer satisfactorily these questions may be a factor in the decreasing number of young men entering the ministry and the increasing number of mature men who are leaving the ministry.

It seems clear from a study of the Scriptures and from the way the Holy Spirit has evidently worked through the centuries that some people are called of God to perform certain distinctive functions within the Christian fellowship. Paul says that it is God's gift that some should be apostles, others prophets, others evangelists, and others pastors and teachers (Eph. 4:11). The purpose of these specifically gifted or called ones is that they might prepare, perfect, and equip the saints, God's people, that they in turn might

29

cooperate with their leaders in the building up of the body of Christ.

We can correctly conclude that every calling or vocation can become holy or sacred through a sense of divine partnership, while we insist at the same time that some people have a unique call to a distinctive task.

We will not increase the holiness or sacredness of other vocations or callings by refusing to acknowledge the unique holiness of God's call to certain church-related vocations. Ultimately the results will be the opposite: there will be a decline in the sense of a sacredness of the so-called secular callings.

The truthfulness of the preceding can be illustrated by the relation of the Lord's Day to the other days of the week. Each day of the week should be made holy for a child of God because of its dedication to the purpose of God in the world. The Lord's Day, however, is uniquely holy.

When an individual or a nation fails to recognize the unique holiness of the Lord's Day, sooner or later the sense of the holiness of the other days will be lost.

Let us retain the contemporary emphasis on God's call to all but at the same time recapture so far as we have lost it the uniqueness of the call of God to some to serve in distinctive ways.

# 9. Who Is the Good Christian?

IT IS UNFORTUNATE that we feel it necessary to insert "good" or "real" as a prefix to Christian. It should be sufficient for one simply to be known as a Christian. But it is not. There are entirely too many "Christians" who are merely nominal Christians.

Many answers are given to the question, "Who is the good Christian?" The following are the major ones.

Some suggest that the good Christian is one who does not cheat, smoke, drink, etc. This is the negative test of the Christian life. This emphasis is particularly prevalent among sectarian groups such as the Pentecostals and among those with a considerable sectarian tinge such as Baptists.

Others would say that the good Christian is one who is faithful to the formal requirements of his faith. He attends the services of his church regularly, he supports its program with at least a tithe of his income.

Still others contend that the supreme test of whether or not one is a good Christian is his work in the church. The good Christian is one who teaches a Sunday school class, works with a youth program, or ministers in and through a mission.

A few people judge the Christian more by his active participation in the life of the community. He may or may not be active in the work of his church, but if he provides leadership for worthy causes in his community he is considered a good Christian.

All of the preceding may and should characterize to varying degrees the good Christian. However, no one of them is the supreme test of a good Christian. Really, some people may make one of these "tests" a substitute for real Christian living.

For a person to comprehend what it means to be a real Christian, he needs to understand the nature of the initial Christian experience. When we became children of God we were brought into a vital life-changing union with the resurrected Christ. We were made "new creatures" in Christ Jesus.

To be a real Christian means to let that which was a poten-
tiality in the initial experience become a living, dynamic reality in
our lives. Another way of expressing the same concept is to say
that the real Christian is one who lets the resurrected Christ live
in him and express himself through him. In other words, we are
real Christians to the degree that we are Christlike.

The preceding means that the supreme test of the Christian life
is positive rather than negative; vital rather than formal. Basically
the Christian life is a relationship, a relationship so deep and
meaningful that all of one's life is influenced by it.

The good Christian will not do certain things, he will be faithful
to the formalities of his faith and will be active in the work of his
church and in wholesome and helpful programs in his community.
The motivation for all these expressions of the Christian life, however, will be love for and gratitude to God for the blessings that
have come through his salvation in Christ.

The whole matter can be summarized by simply saying that the
Christian life flows from within outward. Its source is one's vital
relationship to the living Christ.

## 10. The Measure of a Man

"WHEN GOD measures a man he measures the heart and not the head." Is this statement from a denominational publication correct? Does it contain an element of truth, or does it represent a false antithesis?

It is true that God measures a man primarily by what is within the man rather than by external appearances. His word to Samuel when he was selecting a successor to Saul is an abiding word. He said to Samuel: "The Lord seeth not as man seeth; for man looketh on the outward appearance, but the Lord looketh on the heart" (1 Sam. 16:7). The Lord considers what a man really is and not what he may seem to be.

It is possible that the statement above was an effort to correct the tendency of some to overemphasize native ability and training in the work of the Lord to the neglect of dedication and consistency of life. There may be a sense in which God is more concerned about the size of our hearts than of our heads, but he evidently is most concerned about the dedication of both to his purposes in the world.

There is a possibility that the statement stems from an anti-intellectualism which is still entirely too prevalent among some Christian groups. Some seemingly think that education will undermine faith. It may be that their attitude is derived primarily from the threat that education and the trained mind pose for them. Their faith may be based more on secondhand, hand-me-down ideas and prejudices rather than on meaningful personal experiences. Their faith may be dependent on nonessentials rather than on essentials, on the superficial and incidental rather than on the real and vital.

In contrast, God is evidently not afraid of men with great mental ability. Many of God's big men through the centuries have been men with superior minds. This should mean, among other things, that every child of God should seek to develop his mental capacities to the highest and then dedicate them to the service of God and his fellowman. The head or the mind, as is true of the total personality of man, is a part of his stewardship responsibility.

Our conclusion is that the opening statement may serve a good purpose as a corrective, but as is frequently true of a corrective, it goes too far. Some limiting word should have been inserted such as, "When God measures a man he measures *primarily* the heart and not the head." Or, possibly better: "He measures *both* the heart and the head" or "the heart *as well as* the head."

It seems, however, that God does not measure a man so much by his heart or his head as he does by his moral and spiritual stature. Paul suggests that the work of the apostles, prophets, pastors, and others who perform distinctive functions within the Christian fellowship was to equip God's people. The latter in co-operation with the specially called ones were, among other things, to build up the body of Christ till we all come "to a mature manhood and to a perfect measure of Christ's moral stature" (Eph. 4:13, Williams).

Here is God's supreme measuring stick for a man. How do we measure up when we stand beside the stature of Christ? How tall are we?

## II. A Perplexing Problem

ONE OF LIFE'S most perplexing questions is why many people who do not claim to be Christians seem to do a better job of living the Christian life than many who are Christians, including some who are so-called Christian leaders. The late Karl Barth said that it was to the shame of the church that the will of God "has often been better fulfilled outside the church than in it."

Has this ever bothered you? Have you discovered any reasons why it is so frequently true? I have personally searched for years for a satisfactory explanation. The following may not be entirely adequate, but at least the suggestions have been helpful to me.

It may be that we have not placed enough emphasis in our churches on the positive aspects of Christian living. We have too largely tended to measure the quality of a Christian's life in negative terms—what he does not do—and on the basis of his faithfulness to the formalities of the church—attendance at worship services, support of the church program, etc.

In turn, the tendency on the part of so many church members to judge those inside and outside of the church in formalistic, negative terms contributes to a hypercritical spirit on the part of many church members. Too many of us reject those within and outside of the Christian fellowship who do things that we disapprove of.

Many and possibly most church members have not developed the capacity to separate "the sinner and his sin." If they disapprove or "hate" what a man does, they tend to reject or "hate" him. This limits many of us in our capacity to reach and to minister to the needs of people. We should be able to love people regardless of what they do and even regardless of what they are.

Shifting the emphasis somewhat, what might be called the Christian life of the non-Christian may be partly explained by his background. Many a non-Christian lives on borrowed or overflow religion that has come into his life from a godly father or mother or from some other relative.

Also, there are some non-Christians whose religion is their good works. They substitute works for faith and may never identify with the Christian church. Their motivation may be self-centered or it may be thoroughly unselfish. Theirs may be a humanistic, humanitarian approach to life. They may place a high value on man and hence on their service to man, while ignoring man's relationship to God and their responsibility to God.

There is at least one other possible explanation of the fact that non-Christians frequently outlive professing Christians. Karl Barth suggested that where this happens it is not due to the natural goodness of man. He says, "It is because Jesus, as the One who has risen from the dead and sits at the right hand of God, is in fact the Lord of the whole world who has His servants even where His name is not yet or no longer known or praised."

This suggests that where the work of God is being done we can be sure that it is because God is at work there. This is true regardless of who or what may be the instrument of his will and work.

# 12. One-Issue Christians

THERE ARE one-issue voters. There are also one-issue Christians. That the former exist is unfortunate. The existence of the latter is more unfortunate.

The one-issue Christian may judge his own life on the basis of one particular issue. From his perspective he is right on that issue; hence, he considers himself to be a good Christian. More frequently the one-issue Christian judges other Christians on the basis of one issue. This issue is usually a pet subject of his, one on which he considers himself to be right.

For some the one issue will be in the area of personal morality. For others it will be some phase of social morality. For still others the one issue will be a particular theological doctrine or perspective. Regardless of other things, one is considered a good Christian if he is "right" on that doctrine or regarding that perspective.

Those who select an issue in the area of personal morality may be negative or positive in their approach, but more frequently the former than the latter. If negative, the issue may be swearing, smoking, drinking, or some other comparable issue. If one is free of that habit or "vice" he is good; if not he is bad.

For others the one issue may be in the area of positive personal morality. For example, if one is "honest in his business," "a man of integrity," "a good neighbor," "generous," "kind and considerate," he is judged to be a good man. Whatever the virtue, it is a pet idea of the one-issue Christian. If one is "right" regarding that issue or virtue, he is considered a good Christian.

In the contemporary period the one-issue Christian will frequently concentrate on some particular social issue. The goodness or badness of a Christian will be judged upon the basis of his attitude regarding this one issue.

The issue may be capital punishment, divorce, communism, foreign aid, poverty, race, Red China, unemployment, United Na-

tions, or war. The one-issue Christian judges other Christians on the basis of their position regarding a particular one of these issues. If they are wrong from his perspective on the issue then they are wrong. If they agree with his position then they are right and, hence, are good Christians.

It needs to be emphasized over and over again that there is no single issue that is an adequate test of the genuineness and vitality of one's Christian faith. The ultimate test is how much we are like the living Christ. This means, among other things, that a Christian's life should be judged by the totality of its impact.

One may be right, at least from our perspective, on one issue and yet be entirely wrong on equally important issues. We need to remember that the same thing may be true of us. We all have our blind spots.

Let us in this area as elsewhere do unto others as we would have them do unto us. Let us also remember that one may differ with us on what we consider to be the supreme issue or test of the Christian life, and yet overall he may be a better Christian than we are.

# 13. God and the Trained Mind

GOD WILL USE in a special way the trained mind that is dedicated to his work in the world. This means that the child of God should secure the best training available for the work to which he feels led of the Lord. A part of his total stewardship responsibility includes his mind and its training.

As stewards we are not responsible for ability we do not have or for training beyond our capacity to obtain. God can and frequently does effectively use people with limited abilities and training. These are people who have given to God what they have, and he has multiplied it. God has a place and a ministry for each one of us in harmony with our abilities.

On the other hand, some of us may need to remember that God does not place a premium on ignorance. He does not have a special affinity for the untrained mind. There is a latent anti-intellectualism among some Christian groups that seems at times to think that this is true.

The untrained mind may be used by the Lord; it could be used more effectively if it were trained. This means, among other things, that young people should be encouraged to secure the best training possible and then dedicate that training to the work of God and to the service of their fellowman.

I have never forgotten a statement I heard a number of years ago in chapel: "God has a special affinity for the trained mind." It should be restated that this affinity is not for the trained mind as such but for the dedicated trained mind. Such a mind is capable of doing things for the Lord that otherwise it could not do.

For example, there were many heroes of the faith in the Old Testament, but there was only one Moses. He had been trained in all the learning of the Egyptians and was used in an unusual way by the Lord. In many ways he was God's top man in the Old Testament.

There were many men who contributed significantly to the young Christian movement, but there was only one Paul. He was unusually well trained. It is even possible that Paul would be known today if he had never become a Christian.

Call the roll of the men and women through the centuries who have contributed the most to the Christian movement and to the world in general. You will discover that most of them had superior ability but also superior training.

It does seem that God through the centuries has had a special affinity for the trained mind. We should never forget, however, that the trained mind must be dedicated to the work of God in the world.

Among the early church Fathers there were men such as Origen, Clement of Alexandria, and Augustine—all with superior training. To these might be added later such men as Aquinas, the greatest of the schoolmen, and Luther and Calvin, the chief of the reformers. Still later there were molders of the Christian movement such as Wesley and Edwards.

Call the roll of the outstanding preachers and religious leaders in the contemporary period. Most of them are men with superior ability and training, although a few of them may be largely self-educated.

God still has an affinity for a trained mind, although he will use all of us in his service if we give to him what we have. Everyone of us, with little or great ability, should have a deep desire to give to God the best we have.

# ● III.
# MORALS AND MORALITY

## 14. The New Morality

THE NEW MORALITY has become a favorite topic of conversation among many people, particularly among young people.

It will be a mistake for ministers and workers with youth to ignore, ridicule, or discuss the new morality without special preparation. Abundant materials by both exponents and opponents of the movement are readily available in bookstores and libraries.

An examination of the writings of the originators and advocates of the new morality such as Robinson, Fletcher, Pike, and others may convince us that they provide some helpful insights and emphases.

I can appreciate their positive interpretation of the Christian life and the central place that is given to love. I believe they go too far, however, when they insist that love is the only measure of what is right and good. For them nothing is inherently or intrinsically good except love.

Furthermore, I believe that the emphasis on love is not well balanced. Advocates of the new morality do not give proper attention to love for God, which, after all, is the first commandment. Many of us need to be reminded of the "second like it," but we would insist that love for God is basic. The new morality is too largely man-centered. The biblical ethic and the Christian life in general is primarily God-centered.

Also, love can be made central in the Christian ethic without eliminating some place for rules and principles. We can properly raise the question, "How can one know what love would dictate?" Love needs to be informed and guided, unless one would accept the position of John A. T. Robinson that love "has a built-in moral compass, enabling it to 'home' intuitively upon the deepest need of the other." Who would dare to claim, however, that this has been true in his own personal experience?

Really, the new morality assumes that all of us have a moral and spiritual maturity—an unrealistic assumption. Its exponents like to quote Augustine's famous statement: "Love and do what you please." This may sound beautiful, but whose love approaches closely enough to the divine ideal to make this statement an adequate and safe guide for daily conduct?

The results of the new morality have been especially unfortunate among some young people, particularly college students. "Love" from the perspective of many of them cannot be separated from the romantic conceptions of love.

Also, unfortunately, the more popular proponents of the new morality have predominantly used sex relations to illustrate that love is the only valid absolute in the area of moral conduct. They contend that whatever love would approve is right. They further suggest that this may mean that premarital sex and adultery, under certain circumstances, would be right.

One can easily understand how some immature young people and even mature adults would use such statements to justify or defend their own loose sexual practices.

There is considerable possibility that such individuals fail to understand what "love" really is, particularly love with a distinctly Christian flavor.

# 15. Situation Ethics

THE ADVOCATES of situation ethics, another name for the new morality, suggest that moral obligation is relative *to* the situation. Rules, laws, and principles may be illuminators *of* the situation; they are not authoritative *in* the situation.

This article will not discuss situation ethics in general. It will be restricted to a consideration of the importance of the situation in determining what is right or wrong.

It is unfortunate that the word "situation" has been identified with the new morality. One may differ drastically from the typical situationalist and yet believe that the situation may be an important and in some cases a determinative factor in a time of moral decision.

A biblical example of what might be considered a situational approach is Paul's instruction concerning the eating of meat offered to idols (Rom. 14; 1 Cor. 8). Paul was writing to people facing a particular problem in a particular situation. If we look beneath the surface, however, we will discover some principles that can help us any time we face a decision concerning right or wrong.

One such principle is that a Christian should conform to the culture in which he finds himself except when such conformity would necessitate a compromise of basic moral convictions.

There is another important guiding principle evident in what Paul said. It is clearly suggested that a Christian cannot determine what is right or wrong for him to do without giving consideration to what others think. The effect of what he does on others should be an important factor in his decision. This principle is abidingly relevant and is applicable to widely differing situations.

The preceding correctly implies that an activity that may be right in itself can, because of the situation, become wrong for the child of God. It should be added, however, that any action or activity that is wrong within itself or considered wrong by the child of God cannot be made right for him because of the attitude of others toward it.

The maturing Christian has the right and the responsibility increasingly to make his own decisions concerning what is right and wrong for him to do. This does not mean, however, that the source of authority rests within himself. The ultimate authority is in God. The supreme question for a Christian in any time of decision is, "What is the will of God?" His most difficult and perplexing problems are how he can know the will of God and, once knowing it, how he can do it.

The laws and principles found in the Scriptures can be a major source of help to the Christian in any time of decision. It is his responsibility to interpret and then to apply these laws and principles to his particular situation. Some of these laws and principles may simply be, as the situationalists say, illuminators. Others, because they have been so thoroughly tested and so universally accepted, may speak an authoritative word to the situation.

Also, the child of God should never forget that in every situation he can have the leadership of the Holy Spirit. This source of help is almost totally ignored by contemporary situationalists. One of them (Fletcher) claims that love and reason are the only things that count "when the chips are down."

Without belittling one iota love or reason, it should be added that the Scriptures and the Holy Spirit are the most important sources of help "when the chips are down."

# 16. Our Permissive Society

THERE IS WIDELY prevalent in contemporary America a more or less contagious spirit of permissiveness. This spirit is both a product and a producer of the new morality. There have been reports of unmarried men and women university students who live together. Girls check out of dormitories for overnight or weekends and give their boyfriends' addresses.

The impact of such contemporary permissiveness is felt in practically every area of American life. For example, things are permitted in the news media that were unheard of only a few years ago. Obscenity, nudity, and a frankness that approaches crudeness is prevalent in newspapers, newsmagazines, movies, and on radio and television. Recently a newsmagazine referred to ours as "a Babylonian Age."

The shift to a predominantly permissive society has come with unusual rapidity. It has been suggested that America has changed more in the past year than in the preceding fifty years. Pearl Buck recently said that the people of the United States have changed more than any other people in the world except the Red Chinese.

One phase of our increasingly permissive society is its challenge to traditional values and standards. In some areas there is almost a complete transvaluation of values. Old virtues such as thrift and modesty are considered out of date if not actual sins by many people. Really, sin itself is considered by many to be out of date.

The authority of the home and the church, which are the major protectors and promoters of traditional values, has been sharply decreased. Many people, particularly young people, are drifting without a rudder or a compass. A ship that drifts at sea is a real danger not only to itself but to all other ships.

It would be wise for all of us, young and old, to consider seriously the statement Paul Tillich made to a group of college students. He said: "If you jump out of the experience of mankind, you court

47

tragedy—and you should know it." This tragedy may come not only to the individual but also to society as a whole. It should be remembered that traditional values and standards have a history back of them. Some may need updating, but at least they should be treated with respect.

Is the increasing permissiveness of our society a sign of decay and the approaching collapse of our nation?

It should never be forgotten that periods such as the present one have in the past frequently been a forerunner of the decline and fall of nations and civilizations. This has been particularly true when that permissiveness permeated the area of sex, and today in no area is it more prevalent in than in the area of sex.

It is possible, of course, that the wheel will turn or the pendulum will swing back, at least part of the way. There may be a reaction to the present permissiveness. People may discover that it is not the way of self-fulfillment and genuine happiness. They may conclude that true freedom does not result from no restraint but from the proper restraint.

It seems clear that the reactions within the next few years to our contemporary permissive morality will determine the destiny of our nation for the indefinite future.

# 17. God's Laws:
# Written and Unwritten

LIFE IS GOVERNED by certain basic laws. These are the unwritten laws of God, except as they are written into the nature of man and of the world in which he lives. These are just as much the laws of God as are the written laws found in the Scriptures.

The basic laws are for our good and are valid for man in every age. They do not change with each passing generation. This is true because the nature and needs of man remain basically the same.

Are God's written laws abidingly relevant and valid? It may help us answer this question if we will ask and seek to answer some additional questions. What is the relation of the written laws of God to his unwritten laws or the basic laws of life? Are the formalized, written laws in conformity to and expressive of the basic unwritten laws?

There should be a close relation between the written and unwritten laws since God is the source of both. It is true, of course, that God had to depend on finite men as the channels for the revelation of his written law.

These men, in turn, were limited by the people among whom they lived. Jesus recognized this limitation when he said that it was because of the hardness of the hearts of the people that Moses permitted divorce (Matt. 19:8). Jesus himself went back of the law to the original purpose of the Lawgiver.

The basic laws of life express the original purpose of God and his continuing will for man and the world. Where the written laws of the Old Testament are expressive of the basic laws of God, they also are abidingly relevant and valid.

Some of the Old Testament laws were clearly for the children of Israel at a particular point in their history. For example, we do not consider the ceremonial laws and some of the civil laws as relevant for us today. In contrast, it seems clear that the fundamental moral law of the Old Testament is in harmony with and

49

expressive of the basic laws of God. If this is correct, then the basic moral laws of the Old Testament are applicable to us in the contemporary period. And we should not forget that the Ten Commandments summarize those basic moral laws.

It seems clear that both the fundamental moral laws of the Old Testament and the basic laws of life are given for man's good. This could be the correct interpretation of the statement by Jesus that the Sabbath was made for the good of man and not man for the Sabbath (Mark 2:27).

John says that the commandments of God are not grievous, burdensome, or "too hard for us" (1 John 5:3). Why are they not burdensome or too hard? Because they are provided by God not to suppress us but to lift us, to protect and enrich our lives.

Life is found in its fullest when it is lived in harmony with the basic laws of life and with the written laws of God that are expressive of the basic laws.

I believe it is wise for young people, and older people as well, to remember that God knew what was best for man and for his society when he said, "Thou shalt not commit adultery." So it is with every other basic law of God—written or unwritten.

# 18. Therefore Morality

THE WORD "therefore" usually introduces a truth or statement grounded in or based upon something that has preceded it. In the area of Christian morality the "therefore" usually refers either to the moral nature of God or more specifically to the goodness and grace of God as revealed in his attitude toward and his dealings with man. God is holy; therefore we are to be holy. God loves us; therefore we are to serve him. Christian morality is "therefore morality."

In the Old Testament the "therefore" usually introduces the judgment of God. This judgment in turn is a result of the sinfulness of man. Back of the sinfulness of man and in marked contrast to it are the justice, righteousness, and holiness of God. These and other qualities may not be specifically mentioned, but one or more of them are always in the background as a part of the basis for the judgment of God.

The word "therefore" and the "therefore" concept of morality are particularly prominent in prophets such as Amos and Micah. For example, the former represents God as speaking to the children of Israel as follows: "You only have I known of all the families of the earth." Notice what follows immediately: "therefore I will punish you for all your iniquities" (Amos 3:2).

Micah had a special word for false prophets, for those who made the Lord's people to err, who cried "peace" when there was no peace. The word of Micah was: "Therefore night shall be unto you, that ye shall not have a vision; and it shall be dark unto you" (Micah 3:6).

These and similar statements in the prophets and elsewhere point up a fundamental moral and spiritual law. It is a law that God has written deep into the very nature of things. One way to state the law is as follows: "To whom much is given much will be

51

required." Every favor or blessing from the Lord increases the responsibility of the recipient, whether individual or nation.

The "therefore" motif is just as prevalent in the New Testament. There is a difference, however, in emphasis. In the New Testament the "therefore" usually introduces an exhortation or an appeal. The exhortation is based on what God has done through his grace and goodness. Obligation may be implied, but the appeal is primarily to gratitude. Moses and the prophets commanded; Paul, Peter, and other writers of the New Testament appealed or exhorted.

The "therefore" type of morality is particularly evident in Paul's Epistles, especially in those that are primarily theological in their overall emphasis, such as Romans and Ephesians. In these letters Paul lays down a theological foundation on the basis of which he makes certain moral appeals or exhortations. The transition from the more theological to the more hortatory part of the epistle is introduced with a "therefore" (Rom. 12:1; Eph. 4:1).

The preceding paragraphs correctly imply that morality is not on a sound basis unless it is preceded or introduced with the "therefore" perspective. Distinctly Christian morality is always grounded in what God is, what he has done and is doing.

It should be remembered, however, that just as Christian morality is introduced with a "therefore," one's right relation to God is naturally and inevitably followed with a "therefore" of responsibility.

# 19. Personal and Social Morality

PERSONAL MORALITY and social morality are unfortunately rather sharply divided in the thinking and practice of some Christians and Christian groups. Too frequently one or the other is neglected.

Some Christians who seem to be above reproach regarding personal morality have thoroughly unchristian attitudes toward and relations to some of the more serious moral and social issues. On the other hand, some who have excellent attitudes in the area of social issues are quite careless concerning personal morality.

We should not permit a false alternative to arise. We should not neglect either personal morality or social morality. The choice should be a both/and rather than an either/or.

Many who emphasize rather exclusively personal morality tend to magnify unduly the negative aspects of the Christian life. For them the quality of the Christian's life is measured primarily by what he does not do.

If one will major on the positive aspects of personal morality, it will more or less inevitably move him toward the broader social and moral issues of life. He will see that the positive aspects of the Christian life are expressed in and through relationships. In other words, a positive perspective regarding personal morality will more or less naturally cause one to see that being a Christian means to apply the Christian spirit and Christian teachings to his relations in the home, in his work, play, racial, or cultural group. Put plainly, being a Christian involves the totality of life.

One is not as Christian as he ought to be until he maintains in his personal life, both from a negative and positive perspective, thoroughly Christian moral standards. Neither is he as Christian as he ought to be until he is thoroughly Christian in the broader social relationships of life and until he has an unquestioned Christian perspective concerning all of the major issues that face and frequently plague our society.

Christian groups as well as individuals frequently tend to give primary emphasis either to personal morality or social morality, sometimes to the neglect of the other. Which one receives primary emphasis will be determined largely by whether or not the group, to use a distinction that is frequently made, is a sect or churchly type of group.

In general, a sect type of Christian group tends to separate itself from the world, while the church type tends to make its peace with the world. The sect type tends to major on personal morality; the church type on social morality.

As an example, Baptists, who have a sect background and who still reveal a considerable sect tinge, have tended to major on personal morality. As they move up in the world, however, they are increasingly becoming a church type. This means that it is natural for contemporary Baptists to give a more prominent place to social morality.

With their sect background, which has not been entirely lost, Baptists have an unusual opportunity to work out and to maintain a proper balance between personal morality and social morality.

# ● IV.
# SEX AND SEX RELATIONS

# 20. The Bible and Sex

AN EXAMINATION of the Bible will reveal a number of very important concepts concerning sex. These can provide guidance for us in an age of chaos and confusion. None of these concepts is more significant than the idea that sex as such is a good gift of God. The biblical record says that when "God saw everything that he had made," which included male and female, "behold, it was very good." The sex urge is no more wrong than the desire for food or drink.

The Bible also reveals that sex, as is true of other good gifts of God, can be expressed in hurtful, self-defeating ways. The sex urge can properly be compared to fire. Fire may be used to cook our food and warm our houses, but it can also destroy those houses. We warn our children not to play with fire. Sex should not be played with. Many young people and also older people can testify that, like fire, sex can get out of control.

It is also quite evident from the biblical record that God would restrict the full expression of the sex urge to the relation of husband and wife. The experience of the human race has indicated that this is not an arbitrary requirement. It is best for the husband and wife, for the home they establish, and for society in general.

Evelyn and Sylvanus Duvall, leading contemporary authorities on the family, recently said, "If you want a good marriage you have your sexual intercourse after, and not before, you are married." Most marriage counselors can verify from their counseling experience that waiting until after marriage will pay rich dividends.

The Bible also reveals that any expression of the sex urge other than the normal physical union of husband and wife is contrary to the purposes of God. This not only includes adultery and fornication; it also includes homosexuality and other forms of sexual deviation.

In addition to the preceding, the Bible has some helpful words for married couples. It is quite clear that the Bible considers sexual

57

union within marriage a normal and necessary part of married life. This, which is taken for granted throughout the Scriptures, is plainly stated by Paul (see 1 Cor. 7:3-5).

Furthermore, husbands and wives are to be faithful to one another. The writer of Hebrews says: "Let marriage be held in honor among all, and let the marriage bed be undefiled; for God will judge the immoral and adulterous" (Heb. 13:4, RSV). There is no sin more uniformly or strongly condemned in the Scriptures than sexual unfaithfulness.

Let all, married and unmarried, take seriously the following words of Paul:

God's plan is to make you holy, and that entails first of all a clean cut with sexual immorality. Every one of you should learn to control his body, keeping it pure and treating it with respect, and never regarding it as an instrument for self-gratification, as do pagans with no knowledge of God. You cannot break this rule without in some way cheating your fellow men. And you must remember that God will punish all who do offend in this matter, and we have warned you how we have seen this work out in our experience of life. The calling of God is not to impurity but to the most thorough purity, and anyone who makes light of the matter is not making light of man's ruling but of God's command (1 Thess. 4:3-8, Phillips).

# 21. The Case for Chastity

CAN A VALID CASE be made for chastity in the contemporary period when there is more sexual knowledge and greater sexual freedom than ever before?

It seems clear that the appeal to the fear of pregnancy or of venereal disease is much less effective than formerly. It is possible, however, that these matters are being dismissed too readily. In spite of the widespread use of contraceptives, including "the pill," there are approximately 300,000 babies born annually in the United States out of wedlock. Also, venereal diseases have increased sharply in recent years, particularly among teen-agers.

But what if these more or less negative arguments for chastity could be entirely eliminated? Would there still exist valid reasons for chastity? These are tremendously important questions not only for youth but also for parents, pastors, and workers with youth.

Some young people, particularly the more intelligent ones, are evidently working out answers for themselves. They believe that the freedom of choice which has been given to them is the freedom to say "no" as well as to say "yes," and they believe to say "no" to sex laxness, which is so prevalent, requires more character, courage, and strength of purpose than to say "yes."

As young people search for personally acceptable moral standards, many of them are realizing that the fullest and best life for them lies along the road of discipline and self-control. They increasingly understand that the best things in life are reserved for those who are masters of their appetites rather than mastered by those appetites.

The more fully they understand the sexual nature of man the more clearly they realize the complexity of man. Its full expression involves the total personalities of two people. Many of them also understand that a person, created in the image of God, is never to be used as a mere "thing," an "it," but rather as a "thou"—as

59

another person. All of us should know that when the expression of sex is purely physical and when another person is used as a mere "thing," the experience itself is not satisfying; it is self-defeating.

Let us also never forget that the basic laws that have been written into our natures cannot be violated without paying the price sooner or later. This would be true in the area of sex even if the occasions for the old fears could be entirely removed.

It seems from all the evidence available that chastity before marriage and faithfulness after marriage are good common sense.

# 22. Sex Education in the Public Schools

CONSIDERABLE controversy has arisen concerning the provision of sex instruction by the public schools.

What should be the position of churches and church leaders concerning the controversy?

It is assumed that most of us will agree that proper sex instruction is needed. Most of us realize that children and youth cannot remain ignorant or "innocent," even if such were desirable. They will pick up sex information, accurate and inaccurate, wholesome or unwholesome, from some source.

Parents are the logical ones to give sex instruction to their own children. Unfortunately, however, most parents give little, if any, such instruction.

Churches can and should do much more than they have done in the areas of sex education. Many of them provide no help for parents or children. Very few have a well-planned program of sex education.

Even if all churches provided an adequate program of sex education, which is far from the actual situation, many and possibly most children and youth would be untouched by the program. And since relatively few parents do the job adequately, if at all, it is evident that something is needed in addition to what the churches do or can do. As churches and church leaders formulate their attitude toward sex education in public schools, they should not forget the great host of people who are untouched by the churches.

If proper sex education is important, and we believe it is, then it seems that the public schools must have some place in their programs for it. Otherwise, many youngsters will never receive any instruction except what they pick up from others usually as uninformed as they.

The preceding does not mean a blanket approval of every proposed program of sex instruction in the public schools. Whether

61

such a program is wholesome or unwholesome will be determined by its content and also by the teacher or teachers.

Churches, church leaders, and church members should not oppose sex education as such in the public schools. They should seek to have an effective voice in the formulation and execution of the program of public school sex education. They should be alert to the content of the program and know the one or ones who will teach the course or courses offered.

Furthermore, parents and church leaders should insist that any course in sex education should contain more than mere facts about sex. While it is recognized that teachers in a pluralistic society face some difficulties in expressing value concepts, children and/or youth should be led to recognize that there are basic laws or principles that govern the area of sex.

Someone has suggested that teaching youngsters facts regarding sex without any ethical principles related to sex relations would be like "teaching them to drive a car without giving them the rules of the road." They may become more dangerous to themselves and to others.

# 23. Premarital Pregnancy

WHEN AN UNMARRIED young woman becomes pregnant, several major decisions must be made. Those closely associated with persons involved in premarital pregnancy sometimes can help with guidance from a Christian perspective.

Assuming that the young woman has had relations with only one boy or young man, one of the most immediate problems that they face is whether or not to marry. Also, should they make this decision by themselves or should they consult with their parents, pastor, or some other counselor?

Ordinarily, they should share fully with the parents. Frequently counseling with others will be helpful. It may prevent some tragic mistakes. Parents and other counselors should seek to lead the couple to weigh fully the choices they have. Decisions, however, should ultimately be made by the couple.

It will be a big mistake for parents to force them to marry. There should not be a marriage just "to give a baby a name." Such marriages seldom succeed.

Parents and the young people themselves should know that there are several things that determine whether or not it will be wise for them to marry. A major factor is how much of a chance there is that their marriage will be a sound one. Do they have genuine love and respect for one another? Are there concern for and devotion to the well-being of one another?

There are other questions that may wisely be asked by parents, by pastors, and by the young people themselves. What is the attitude of the young man and the young woman toward the pregnancy? Does each reveal a willingness to accept his or her part of the responsibility? Or is there a tendency to blame the other? Is there present on the part of both a real sense of repentance and at the same time a spirit of forgiveness?

The supremely important question to be asked by all who are

involved, directly or indirectly, in a premarital pregnancy is: "What will be best for the child?"

The pastor will frequently have an opportunity to speak a word for the child. This opportunity may come when the parents consult with him or when the young woman or the couple come to him.

If he is asked to perform the marriage ceremony, that will give him another chance to speak for the child. For the sake of the latter as well as for the sake of the young people involved he may decide to decline to perform the marriage ceremony.

I personally believe that he will be justified in performing the ceremony for such a couple only if after one or more conferences with them he is persuaded that they have a reasonably good chance of founding a home on a solid basis and of providing a wholesome environment for the child.

If the couple decides not to marry, the pastor will frequently have an opportunity to counsel with all concerned about homes for unwed mothers. He may also be asked about the wisest procedures concerning the child. Should the child be retained by the mother, or be adopted by a member of the family or by someone unknown to them?

Primary consideration should be given to what is best for the child. In the majority of cases it will be best from the child's perspective for him to be adopted by someone unknown to the family.

## 24. Venereal Disease

"THERE IS a silent epidemic in the land." This was the opening sentence in a recent article on venereal disease in a daily paper.

In recent years there has been a marked increase in cases of syphilis and gonorrhea, with 100,000 new cases of syphilis and 400,000 of gonorrhea in the United States in a single year. Furthermore, it is estimated that only one in four cases of syphilis and not more than one in ten cases of gonorrhea are reported.

The United States Public Health Service estimates that there are at least 800,000 persons in this country who are in need of treatment for syphilis. If these go untreated, the Health Service says that one in thirteen will develop heart disease, one in twenty-five will be crippled, one in forty-four will develop syphilitic insanity, and one in two hundred will become blind.

The American Medical Association has recently stated that "venereal disease is spreading so rapidly that it now represents the nation's most urgent communicable disease problem."

The most rapid increase in venereal disease in recent years has been among teen-agers. Teen-agers and adults should know that many authorities claim that venereal disease is the most communicable disease of mankind. It is communicable, however, only through skin contact.

It has been suggested that the only way to avoid venereal disease is to steer clear of venereal disease carriers. The added word is: "Who can be sure who that is?" This is one valid reason for premarital chastity and postmarital faithfulness.

Unfortunately, many Christians are a part of "a conspiracy of silence" regarding venereal disease. They think it should not be discussed "in polite society." It should be recognized, however, that there is nothing polite about the way venereal disease operates. It is no respecter of persons. It is found among all classes and colors. Even innocent babies can be infected before birth by a mother who has venereal disease.

What are the reasons for the recent upsurge in venereal disease? One writer has placed the blame primarily on the war in Vietnam. Another, a doctor, says that the "pill" must share the responsibility. He suggests that married and unmarried need to remember that "the pill does not prevent venereal disease." Another doctor has suggested that the "boundaries of sexual freedom have blurred." A public health official recently said that "one of the real reasons" for the marked increase in venereal disease among teen-agers is the breakdown in morals in the home, school, and church.

The latter means, among other things, that these three institutions have important contributions to make to the meeting of the challenge of venereal disease. One contribution that the Christian home and church can make is to seek to build into the lives of young people some relevant basic convictions.

Parents and workers with youth should inform themselves concerning venereal disease. They can secure pamphlets from their county or state department of health. The church librarian should consider having available pamphlets or books for circulation among parents and teen-agers.

# ● V.
# LIFE AND DEATH

# 25. Abortion

THERE ARE important moral and ethical issues involved in the contemporary effort to modify existing abortion laws. Christians should be alert to these issues and should seek to think through them to a defensible Christian position.

At the present time most states permit "induced termination of pregnancy" only when the life of the mother is endangered. A few states permit abortion to protect the "health and safety" of the mother. Three states prohibit "unlawful abortion" with no further clarification. Four or five states have recently modified and liberalized their laws regarding abortion. In many other states the legislatures have considered or are considering the revision of their abortion laws.

The abortion laws in some states possibly should be revised. With proper safeguards, abortion might be permitted in the case of incest or rape. It is possible that the interpretation of the "health of the mother" should be broadened to include mental as well as physical health.

The remainder of this article, however, will be limited to a consideration of the suggestion that abortion be permitted when "there is documented evidence that the infant may be born with incapacitating physical deformity or mental deficiency."

The preceding is included in a statement on abortion approved by the American Medical Association. The same idea is included in a law proposed by the American Law Institute. I have great respect for doctors and lawyers, but I would like to ask the nature of the "documented evidence." Also, how much of a chance is there for an error in judgment?

Notice that the statement says "may be born" rather than "will be born." One group of doctors has said that only rarely can medical science predict with certainty that a child will be defective.

Furthermore, what is to be the definition of "incapacitating"?

What type of physical deformity and what degree of mental deficiency would incapacitate the child.

Many parents of the handicapped can join me in testifying that the "incapacitated" son or daughter has brought many rich blessings to their lives. Pearl Buck, in a recent statement, suggested that a retarded child or handicapped person brings his or her own "gift of life, even to the life of normal human beings."

How would the approval of the aborting of infants with "incapacitating physical deformity or mental deficiency" affect our society? One of the brightest spots in our culture is what is done for the physically handicapped and mentally retarded children among us.

There is an additional question that constantly bothers me: If we justify the abortion of the potentially handicapped child, would not the next logical step be the justification of the termination of life for the incurably ill and for the old and "useless"? If life can be artificially terminated at one end, can it not just as logically be terminated at the other end?

# 26. Death with Dignity

A FRIEND of mine passed away after a long illness. The doctors concluded months before his death that the illness was terminal. Yet he was kept alive for several weeks by artificial means. This cost the family thousands of dollars.

This experience and similar incidents raise questions that should be answered. Should one whose illness is definitely terminal be kept alive by artificial means—medication, tubes, etc.?

Some people contend that the doctor's oath binds him to preserve life and not to take it. Some even suggest that the physician is under obligation to keep one alive as long as possible. Others say that his oath simply means that he is not to take life; he is not to practice positive euthanasia.

The latter is the correct interpretation. The only statement in the oath that relates to this matter is as follows: "I will give no deadly medicine to any one if asked, nor suggest any such counsel."

Another argument made by some people for the artificial continuation of life is the fact that a doctor's diagnosis may be wrong. He may consider a case terminal when it is not. For one thing, he has no way to measure a particular patient's will to live.

Furthermore, some insist that a doctor cannot predict how God will work in a particular case. Therefore, so they reason, the doctor should use every skill and technique available to keep one alive.

There are others, including some doctors, who claim that the medical profession may learn a great deal by using artificial methods to keep a patient alive. If this is a valid reason for using various means of extending life in terminal cases, we do not believe the family should have to pay the bill. The doctor, the hospital, the medical society, the government, or some charitable foundation should relieve the family of the tremendous expense frequently involved.

There is a possibility that one reason for efforts to keep people

alive as long as possible is the fear of death. This may be under-
standable for non-Christians, but it is hard to understand why
Christians should fear death personally or for their loved ones
who are Christians. After all, death is inevitable. There are limits
to how long it can be postponed.

Members of the family, who should have a major voice regarding any decision that is made, should be fully informed regarding
possible costs. While the cost should not be the deciding factor in
any decision that is made, it may properly be a major factor at
least for families with limited financial resources.

The one whose voice should speak the loudest is the patient
himself. This is particularly true if he decides against the artificial continuance of his life. Such a decision should be made while
he is still in full control of his faculties.

If he wishes to be permitted "to die with dignity" he should let
his family and his doctor know. Those wishes should be respected.
We have such an understanding in our household. There is no
question about our understanding being carried out by the family
and by the family physician.

Why should any of us want to hold on to life when our days of usefulness are over? Why should we want to live any longer when it would simply add to the burdens of loved ones and friends?

Why not go on and be with the Lord? After all, Paul said, "For me to live is Christ, and to die is gain" (Phil. 1:21, KJV). Do we really believe this or have we been teaching and preaching something we have not believed?

# 27. Capital Punishment

CAPITAL PUNISHMENT has been debated for many years. Christians are rather sharply divided regarding it.

The general trend in the United States has been away from capital punishment. There has been a decrease in the crimes that are punishable by death. Murder is the only capital offense in most states, although some retain it as punishment for rape, robbery, and arson.

Ramsay Clark, former Attorney General of the United States, recently suggested that capital punishment for federal offenses should be abolished. He said that it would be one more step out of barbarism.

The American Institute of Public Opinion recently released a report showing that the percentage of people approving the death penalty for persons convicted of murder had decreased from 68 percent in 1953 to 51 percent in 1960 and 49 percent in 1966.

The number of convicted murderers who have been executed in recent years has noticeably decreased. In 1936 there were 194 executions in the United States; thirty years later there was only one execution in the entire country. As the number executed has decreased, the number in "death row" awaiting execution has sharply increased. California recently reported over seventy men awaiting execution, while Florida had fifty in death row. In addition there were many more in county jails who had been assessed the death penalty.

Several states have abolished capital punishment. A recent Associated Press report said that thirteen states had either abolished it or had so restricted it as to make it almost nonexistent. There are approximately seventy (70) foreign countries that have abolished the death penalty.

Contrary to the contention of the defenders of capital punishment, it is not an effective deterrent to crime. There is little if any evidence of an increase in capital offenses in states or countries that have abolished capital punishment. One report reveals that the five states that most frequently assess the death penalty have the highest murder rates.

There are several additional arguments against the death penalty. One of the strongest is the discriminatory way in which it is applied. Who are the ones who are executed? In the main, they are the poor or the underprivileged of society. To an unusual degree, they belong to the minority peoples of our culture.

Still another reason for the abolition of capital punishment is the fact that when carried out there is no way to correct an error. There have been cases where a man has been executed and later it was discovered that he was innocent. The fact that a judge and a jury may make a mistake should raise serious questions about capital punishment.

What is needed in contemporary America is a more enlightened and effective penal system. The emphasis should be primarily remedial rather than punitive. If one cannot be reformed so as to become again a useful citizen, then he should be separated from society for the remainder of his life.

There is no place for capital punishment in a remedially oriented penal system.

# 28. The Bible
## and Capital Punishment

THE BIBLE has been appealed to by some who oppose capital punishment but particularly by those who defend it.

The Old Testament is used, in the main, by the latter. What do we find in the Old Testament? There are fifteen to twenty offenses that are punishable by death. Would those who use the Bible to defend capital punishment assess the death penalty for all of those offenses?

As one would expect, premeditated murder was punishable by death (Gen. 9:6; Ex. 21:12), although six cities of refuge were provided for those who had killed another "unawares" or "without enmity" (Num. 35:9-34). The death penalty was also assessed for one who stole a man and sold him (Ex. 21:16).

There were two offenses against parents that were punishable by death: smiting or striking (Ex. 21:15) and cursing (Ex. 21:17).

Certain sexual acts were capital offenses. An adulterous relation between a man and another man's wife meant death for both (Lev. 20:10; Deut. 22:22). If a husband accused his wife of not being a virgin when he took her and "the tokens of her virginity be not found for the damsel" she was to be stoned to death (Deut. 22:13-21).

If a man had relations with a betrothed virgin in the city both were to be put to death (Deut. 22:23-24)—if in the field, the man alone was to be put to death. In the latter case it was assumed that the damsel cried for help and no one heard her (Deut. 22:25-27).

Incest (Lev. 20:11-12, 14) and homosexuality (Lev. 20:13) were punishable by death; this was also true of lying with a beast (Ex. 22:19), which applied to women as well as men (Lev. 20:15-16).

Certain religious transgressions were considered capital offenses. This was true of one who defiled the sabbath, including doing any

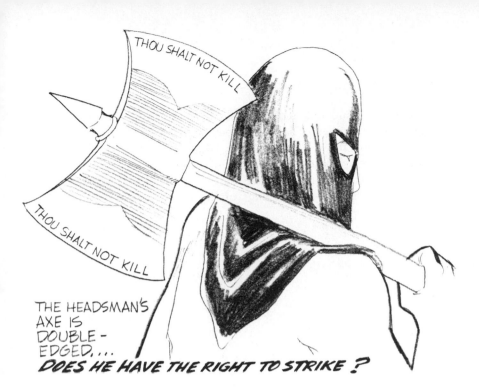

THE HEADSMAN'S AXE IS DOUBLE-EDGED, ...

DOES HE HAVE THE RIGHT TO STRIKE ?

work on the sabbath day (Ex. 31:14-15; cf. 35:2). One man was actually stoned to death for gathering sticks on the sabbath (Num. 15:32-36).

A prophet or a "dreamer of dreams" who would lead the people to worship false gods (Deut. 13:5), one who would entice others to "serve other gods" (Deut. 13:6-10), and those who worshiped other gods (Deut. 17:2-5) were to be put to death. The same was true of those who gave their children to Molech in sacrifice (Lev. 20:2) or who blasphemed God (Lev. 24:16).

The stranger who came near to the Tabernacle when it was being set up by the Levites (Num. 1:51) or when the sons of Aaron were ministering in it (Num. 3:10, 38) was to be put to death.

There was a provision for the death penalty for a witch (Ex. 22:18) or one who had a familiar spirit or was a wizard (Lev. 20:27).

Surely no one in the contemporary period would advocate capital punishment for all of the preceding offenses. Personally, I do not believe we can wisely or correctly use what we find in the Bible as justification for capital punishment in our day.

The severity of the punishment found in the Old Testament

needs to be evaluated and understood in the light of that day. Other than the cities of refuge, a penal system was nonexistent.

Furthermore, the teachings of the Old Testament should be interpreted and evaluated in the light of the fuller revelation found in the New Testament. I believe that capital punishment violates the spirit and the basic teachings of the New Testament.

# ● VI.
# THE FAMILY

WEDDING BAND...

# 29. Preparing
## Our Children for Life

A GROUP of missionaries asked me to discuss with them what they could do to prepare their children for return to the States to complete their education. The following is an adaptation of the discussion with the missionaries.

1. Build a closely knit family unit. Father, mother, and children should be genuinely devoted to one another. They should share play, work, and worship.

2. Cultivate a close relationship with children from their earliest days. Parents cannot wait until children are teen-agers to prepare them for life. Regardless of how much attention we give to them as teen-agers it will not compensate for our failure to give time and attention to them in their earlier years.

3. Provide in the home an atmosphere of love and discipline for the growing child, and let us remember that there is no necessary conflict between the two. When discipline is properly administered it can and will be an expression of love.

4. Hold a tight but gentle rein on the maturing youngster. Contrary to what many people think, he not only needs but he also wants some limits set for him.

5. Gradually shift control to the son or daughter. This is one of the most difficult and delicate tasks of parents. The maturing child must increasingly make his own decisions if he is to be prepared for life.

6. Build into the lives of children basic moral and religious principles, including the fact that the moral and the religious are integral parts of one another. When our children leave home, the principles we have built into their lives, along with our prayers, will be our chief hope for them.

7. Surround the children in the home with a wholesomely stimulating intellectual and spiritual environment in which they will develop normally and naturally.

8. Do not insist that children should or should not do certain things simply because their parents are missionaries or are in some other church-related vocation. If we press this reason or argument it may contribute to the rebellion of our children, particularly when they leave home.

9. Be positive more than negative in approach to and interpretation of the Christian life. The negatives or the "thou shalt nots" have a continuing contribution to make to the preparation of our children for life, but it is important for them to understand that the chief test of the Christian is positive: how much he exemplifies in his life the teachings and spirit of Christ.

10. Be careful about our attitude toward the work we are doing for the Lord, whether as missionary, pastor, deacon, teacher, etc. If we are not happy in our work it will tend to affect the attitude of our children toward the Lord and his work.

11. Beware of criticism in the presence of immature children of fellow missionaries, the denomination and its program, or our church and its leadership. If there are problems that we need to discuss, let us do so when the children are absent or asleep.

12. Be genuine and sincere in the expressions of our religious life. It is doubtful if any one thing will contribute more to the strength and stability of character of our children when they leave home than for them to know that, in spite of our weaknesses, we are sincere Christians.

# 30. Discipline in the Home

ONE OF THE MOST difficult and delicate tasks of parents is the discipline of their children. Some may be too severe, others may be entirely too lax or easy, while many and possibly most are inconsistent.

Unfortunately the father and mother frequently differ regarding the discipline of the children. If this is true they should work out their differences in private and not in the presence of the children.

An understanding of the purpose of discipline will help parents to know when and how to discipline their children. From the viewpoint of the child, the purpose of discipline is that he may mature into a person who can discipline himself. In order for this to be accomplished, the child must understand the purpose of the discipline and believe in its fairness.

Also, children cannot mature into well-disciplined persons unless they are led increasingly to make their own decisions. The effective shifting of authority from parents to growing children is one of life's most significant achievements.

Another purpose of discipline is the maturing of law-abiding citizens. The home more than any other agency or institution will determine whether or not society has such citizens. Unless parents in the home teach respect for authority and for those who exercise that authority, society will not have citizens who respect the law or those who enforce the law.

There are a number of things that will help to make discipline more effective. Fairness of the punishment has been mentioned. The child should be convinced that the discipline or punishment is not excessive for the particular violation.

The child should also understand the reason for the discipline. This ordinarily requires the parent to be calm and to talk the matter over with the child. Seldom is a parent justified in punishing a child when he is angry.

There are few things more important in discipline than consistency. Too frequently parents let how they feel at the moment determine whether or not they discipline a child. The effectiveness of punishment depends more on its consistency and the child's understanding the reason for the punishment than on its severity.

Where does physical punishment fit into the whole picture of discipline? Too many parents practically equate physical punishment and discipline. There are many other methods of discipline: talking to a child, withdrawal of privileges, restriction of activities, etc. The method used should be adapted to the child as well as to the offense.

At least one or two additional words should be addressed to parents. They cannot expect to have well-disciplined children unless they themselves are well-disciplined. Also, when properly understood, discipline includes much more than punishment. The moral and spiritual principles and ideals that are built into the lives of growing children will be major factors in disciplining their lives. Also, the atmosphere of or the spirit in the home will make a major contribution.

The best discipline is largely unconscious, primarily caught rather than taught.

## 31. The Working Wife

THE TERM "the working wife" refers to wives who work outside the home, of whom there are an increasing number. A relatively recent report said that women composed 35 percent of the working force in the United States.

The same report suggested that a few decades ago the average working woman was single and twenty-eight years of age. In contrast, she is now forty-one and has two children.

Why are so many wives and mothers a part of the "working force"? There are some who work to get away from the "boredom" of housework. The vast majority of them work, however, because they believe additional income is needed for their families. The younger wives frequently work to help husbands complete their education or to enable the two of them to get established.

Many mothers work to help with the increasing expenses of a growing family, to help with the college education of children, or to assist with the cost of caring for aged or aging parents. Still others work to get out of debt or simply to provide better living for the family.

It may be wise for the working wife and/or mother to analyze carefully the financial contributions her working makes to the family. How much will be left after she pays for transportation, lunches, additional clothes that may be needed, and such household help as she will have to have? She may discover that her additional income does not amount to as much as she had anticipated.

Several things should be done if possible where the husband and wife both work. They should have work schedules that will enable them to have as much time as possible together at home. If possible, vacations should be taken at the same time.

The income of both should be considered family income. There should be joint planning of the family budget. They should seek to meet regular family expenses from the husband's income and

use the wife's for specials such as debts, furniture, savings, etc. This will mean that if and when she decides to quit work, they will not have the painful and difficult experience of adjusting to a lower standard of living.

There are particular problems when there are children in the home. Unless it is absolutely necessary for the mother to work, she should not do so before the children start to school. After the children are all in school it will be good if the mother can be present when the children leave for and return from school. Even teenagers often need the sense of security that comes from a mother who sees them off to school and who will be there to welcome them when they come in from school.

After the children are out of the home, in college or at work, the mother would be freer to work, but she should consider the effect of her working on her and on her husband.

It seems to me that there is one safe, universal rule that can be laid down concerning the working wife: unless absolutely necessary she should not work outside the home if it will mean the neglect of her home, her husband, and her children.

# 32. Divorce and Sin

A PROPER understanding of the biblical conception of marriage and the home on the one hand, and of sin on the other hand will convince one that sin is involved in every divorce.

The Bible clearly reveals that God's original purpose and his ultimate ideal for the home was and is the union of one man and one woman as husband and wife for life. On the other hand, one of the Hebrew words for sin in the Old Testament and a comparable Greek word in the New Testament mean "to miss the mark." Any time an individual or a God-ordained institution misses the mark that God has set, it is sin.

Since God's mark or purpose for the home was and is the lifetime union of husband and wife, divorce on any grounds involves sin. In addition, there are sins of various kinds that may contribute to the sin of divorce.

Pastors and other marriage counselors know that when a divorce has occurred or is threatened, with rare exceptions, both husband and wife must share in the responsibility for the divorce. There is seldom if ever a completely innocent party in a conflict that leads to divorce. Most of the responsibility may be on one side or the other, but both have sinned and come short of the purposes of God—they have "missed the mark."

Either husband or wife may sin simply by not being willing to make adjustments, by being unwilling to work as hard as he or she should to make the marriage succeed. In other words, the husband and wife should be reminded that there are sins of omission as well as of commission.

Also, one or both partners may sin by refusing to acknowledge his or her responsibility for the failure of their marriage. It is a sin to shift to others the responsibility that properly belongs to us.

Closely akin to the preceding is the fact that repentance and forgiveness are essential in any mutually satisfying human relations. There is no relationship where these are more important than in the home. Insofar as a lack of either or both of these has been a factor in the divorce, sin is involved.

One other word needs to be said about sin and divorce. The sin of divorce and the sins that contribute to divorce are not unpardonable sins. This sin and these sins, like other sins, can be forgiven. Our heavenly Father can and wants to forgive every sin, including the sin of divorce. The latter is true regardless of the reason for the divorce.

If men and women who have been divorced are to have the Father's forgiveness they must seek it. One factor in seeking God's forgiveness is genuine repentance for sins that have been factors in the divorce and repentance for the divorce itself. The forgiveness that is available from God if one will genuinely repent must be appropriated.

Entirely too many Christian men and women seemingly do not believe that God has forgiven them when the basic problem is that they have not forgiven themselves. And there is no forgiveness of self without a prior acknowledgment of guilt.

# 33. Adultery and Divorce

THIS ARTICLE will be restricted to a consideration of three questions concerning the relation of adultery and divorce.

The first question is: "Does one commit adultery when he gets a divorce or only when he remarries?"

Without encouraging anyone to take divorce lightly, it seems relatively clear that adultery occurs only when one remarries. The words of Jesus were, "The man who divorces his wife and marries another woman commits adultery against his wife" (Mark 10:11).

Another question is: "Does the so-called innocent party in a divorce based on adultery (Matt. 19:9) have the right to marry again or would such a marriage be adulterous?"

Notice the word "so-called." It is doubtful if there is ever a completely innocent party in a divorce, even when the ground for the divorce is adultery. It may be that only the husband or the wife has been guilty of overt physical adultery. And while no one should be excused for committing adultery, the mate in many cases must share to some degree the guilt.

It does seem, however, that the so-called innocent party can marry again without committing adultery. This conclusion is based to some degree on the nature of marriage. When a husband and wife have physical union they become one or one flesh. When either has sexual intercourse with another, the original union is broken.

Furthermore, it seems that the most logical interpretation of the teachings of Jesus as reported in Matthew 19:9 is that one who had not been unfaithful did not commit adultery by marrying another.

It is doubtful, however, if the so-called innocent party has the right to remarry unless he or she sincerely acknowledges some responsibility for the divorce, genuinely repents of his or her sin, and forgives the mate for his or her part of the tragic experience.

There is still another question that frequently disturbs sincere searching Christian husbands and wives. The question is, "When one has divorced a companion on any basis other than adultery and marries again, is he or she living in adultery with the present mate?" This question becomes unusually disturbing to some husbands and wives who become Christians or who have an awakening Christian experience after their divorce and remarriage.

Some things can be said that may be of help to those who are honestly seeking an answer to this question. Many of them are in situations that cannot be basically changed. It would be unwise if not impossible to go back and undo the mistakes of the past. The best thing, and frequently the only wise thing, is to ask God to forgive the mistakes of the past and start from where they are, seeking to live as genuine a Christian life as possible. When they ask the Lord to forgive them, they should really believe that he can and will forgive the sin of divorce and adultery just as he can and will forgive any other sin.

There is also a possibility that the adultery that attends such remarriage is a one-act offense rather than a continuing one. A new union is formed when the husband and wife in the new marriage have physical relations. This has made them one. After that it would be adultery for them to be unfaithful to one another.

The main thing is for one who faces this problem to have a deep conviction that God can take care of any problem that they may have regarding their relations with their present husband or wife.

# 34. Pastors and the Divorced

THE PASTOR should maintain a wholesome pastoral relationship to divorced men and women both in his congregation and in the community. We will restrict this discussion, however, to whether or not a pastor should perform the wedding ceremony for the divorced.

There are four rather well-defined positions maintained by pastors. Each minister should think and pray through to a position that he can conscientiously defend and can maintain with reasonable consistency.

Some pastors insist that a minister is simply acting as an agent of the state when he performs a marriage ceremony. Hence, they will perform the ceremony for anyone who comes to them with a marriage license.

This does not seem to me to be a defensible Christian position. A pastor is not merely an agent of the state when he performs a marriage ceremony; he is also and primarily a minister of God. As a minister he is responsible to God for what he does in every area and activity of his life.

Other pastors go to the opposite extreme: They will not perform the marriage ceremony for anyone who has been divorced. Some do not believe the Scriptures justify marriage after divorce. Others contend that this is the most practical position for them. They say that they cannot in good conscience perform the ceremony for all divorced and it is difficult, if not impossible, for them to discriminate wisely. They believe that the best policy for them is not to perform the ceremony for any who have been divorced. They also suggest that this policy makes it unnecessary to explain why they will perform the ceremony for some who have been divorced and not for others.

A third position maintained by some pastors is that they will perform the ceremony only for those who have what is called scriptural grounds for divorce: fornication or unchastity. Most of those who follow this policy base their position on a belief that Matthew 19:9 would permit remarriage for the so-called "innocent party" where adultery has been committed.

A fourth position, rather widely practiced by pastors, is that every marriage involving a divorced person should be treated as an individual case. In other words, whether or not the pastor will perform the ceremony will depend on whether or not he is convinced that the couple has a good chance of establishing a stable Christian home.

Any pastor who follows this last policy must be willing to take the time for one or more conferences with the couple before agreeing to perform the ceremony. Without such conferences he can seldom if ever know whether or not he should perform the ceremony.

I am not an ordained minister and have never performed a marriage ceremony. For many years, however, I suggested in my classes and elsewhere that if I were a pastor I would not perform the ceremony for anyone who had been divorced.

In recent years, my position has changed considerably. I believe now that I would follow the last position outlined: make each case an individual case. Several factors have contributed to this change. A major one has been the rather extensive counseling I have done through the years, including many people who have been divorced. Also, as I have matured in years, wisely or unwisely, I have become more sympathetic and less judgmental of people who have made tragic mistakes regarding marriage. Furthermore, I am less legalistic in my interpretation of the teachings of the Scriptures concerning divorce and remarriage.

# ● VII.
# THE CHURCH

# 35. Churches and Tax Exemption

Is IT CONSISTENT with the separation theory for churches to be exempt from taxation? Some contend that it is the only practice consistent with the separation of church and state. They suggest that the power to tax is the power to control. Others insist that this argument is mere rationalization.

It is also suggested that the exemption from taxation of church property is a recognition by the government of the valuable and distinctive contribution of the churches to the general welfare.

Whatever the reasons for the exemption, it has been the traditional practice in our nation and evidently will be for the indefinite future. There are, however, many citizens, including some sincere churchmen, who are raising questions concerning the practice.

I do not claim to be a tax expert, but it does seem to me that we need to give some attention to the tax-exempt status of churches and church-related agencies and institutions.

I personally believe that the only property of local churches that should be tax exempt should be the building or buildings that are used for worship and educational purposes. If the church has revenue-producing property, it certainly should be taxed. This would include houses or business properties that are rented.

The preceding would also mean that the houses provided by the church for members of the church staff, including the pastor, would be taxed. These taxes might be paid by the church or by the staff members themselves. Having the staff pay their own taxes would enable them to identify more fully with the members of the church.

Also, I believe it would be proper for the church to pay an agreed amount to the county or city for fire and police protection. Why should citizens who are not members of the church or of any church be taxed to provide protection for churches?

Denominational agencies and institutions may need to review their policies regarding taxation. Let their trustees and administrators be sure that they do not abuse their present tax-exempt status. Surely no church or denominational agency or institution should ever enter into an agreement that would enable an individual or a business concern to evade taxes. I am referring here to deals where the individual or company will give a business to a church or denominational agency with the understanding that it will be leased back to the original operators.

Taxes should be paid on all revenue-producing property by boards, benevolent institutions, colleges, seminaries, and other denominational agencies. Dormitories could be an exception to this rule, but only if the rent charged cares simply for liquidation and/or depreciation. Any time an institution, through apartments or housing, becomes competitive with legitimate business interests in the community, it should pay the same taxes as its competitors. Certainly any property held for investment purposes should be taxed.

Let church-related institutions be more concerned with what is fair and right than they are with what will be most advantageous to them.

## 36. The Church:
## Gathered and Scattered

THE CONTEMPORARY church has many critics. Some of them speak from within the church; others from without. Some are sympathetic and constructive; others are cynical, sarcastic, and destructive. Whatever the source or the spirit of the criticism, it will be wise for church leaders to evaluate objectively every criticism.

Many critics of the institutional church correctly suggest that it is too exclusively concerned about itself: its buildings, its organization, its program, and its prestige in the world. They contend that the church is in the world to serve. Some of them insist that to serve effectively, the church must be a scattered rather than a gathered church.

In reality, the church needs to be and is both a gathered and a scattered church. The effectiveness of its ministry in and to the world will depend on how well it keeps in balance these two aspects of its life: gathered from the world and in turn scattered to and for the world.

This means, among other things, that there still may be an important place for the so-called institutionalized church so frequently ridiculed by its critics.

The church, as the people of God, is first gathered by the Lord from the world and separated unto him and his purposes. We, through our efforts, may add names to the rolls of our churches but God alone can add them to the church. We are to be a holy people, dedicated to his purposes in the world.

The church is not only composed of those who have been gathered *by* the Lord, its members should also periodically be gathered together *for* the Lord. We should come together for fellowship with one another and with the Lord. We need to be instructed in the Word and work of the Lord. We need to join together in the worship of the Lord. In the words of the writer of Hebrews, we should not forsake the assembling of ourselves together.

It is the very nature of the church to be a scattered as well as a gathered church. The church is wherever we, its members, are on Monday through Saturday as well as on Sunday. We are our church where we live, work, and play as well as where we worship. In other words, all we need to do to make a greater impact for God on the world is for us to recognize that we are the scattered church and then to live a more consistent Christian life in the world.

Let us never forget, however, that we should gather regularly with fellow church members. Our inner spiritual resources need to be renewed. We need a deepened sense of the presence of the Lord and a renewed dedication to his work in the church and in the world.

We can sum up by saying that we have been gathered as a church from the world by the Lord, and in turn we are scattered by him to do his work in the world. For the most effective ministry in and to the world, we will need to maintain in our lives a constant interplay of gathering and scattering.

# 37. Sins in the Sanctuary

It MAY SOUND sacrilegious to speak of sins in the sanctuary. It should be remembered, however, that Jesus cleansed the temple. It is possible that contemporary churches need to be cleansed.

Our church buildings have been dedicated to God and to his worship. How thoroughly are they being used to fulfill his purposes? The sanctuary stands in the community as a symbol of God's presence among the people. Do the people recognize it as such a symbol? Whether or not they do will be determined largely by the prevalence or absence of certain sins in the sanctuary.

One sin that has to be guarded against is a worldly pride in the building itself. Certainly a church should provide a worthy house for the Lord, but we need to watch or an unworthy pride will creep in. This pride frequently expresses itself in a boastful parade of the cost of the building. There may also be pride in some of the luxuries that add nothing to efficiency.

Pride in the building may repel the very people the church needs most to reach. It is even possible that some members of the church will prefer for certain types of people not to be reached by the church. The latter may be an expression of self-satisfaction and self-centeredness.

Closely akin to, if not identical with, the preceding is the spirit of self-righteousness. This was the only sin specifically condemned by Jesus. It was the sin of the Pharisees, the most "religious" people of that day.

Too many who regularly attend the services in our sanctuaries secretly if not openly pray the prayer of the Pharisee: "I thank you, God, that I am not . . . like everybody else" (Luke 18:11). He went on to inform the Lord what a good man he was. We need to have, even in the sanctuary, the spirit of the publican who prayed: "O God, have pity on me, a sinner" (Luke 18:13).

One of the besetting sins of those of us who regularly attend the

services of our churches is a failure to recognize our sinfulness. Too many of us in the sanctuary do not recognize that we all "like sheep have gone astray" (Isa. 53:6), that all of us "have sinned and come short of the glory of God" (Rom. 3:23, KJV).

Also, entirely too many of us go from the sanctuary unchanged. This is a sin. We supposedly came to worship God. We can be sure that if we are not changed when we leave his house, we have not worshiped him.

If we, through genuine worship, have had a vision of the God revealed in the Scriptures, then we will go out of the sanctuary to attempt to make that vision a reality in the world. If we do not go into the world, it is a sin. If we go with any purpose other than to serve, it is also a sin.

## 38. Tendencies That Threaten

WE IN AMERICA should be grateful to God for his evident blessings on the work of our churches. But we should be alert to tendencies that threaten to reduce, if not to destroy, their effectiveness.

First, there is a tendency for the churches of many denominations to move up the economic ladder and to move away from the common people. The movement upward seems to be inevitable. The movement away from the common people is not. It is the latter that is a threat to many church groups.

The strength of some major church and denominational groups has been among the laboring people. They must continue to maintain a good rapport with the masses of working people if they are to have an effective voice in shaping the future. The restless masses are doing more to determine the direction of the contemporary world than any other group.

If these church groups are to counteract the tendency to move away from the common people, they must honor the small church as much as the large church, the poor church as much as the rich church, and the "working people's church" as much as "the professional and business people's church."

Second, there seems to be a tendency for most churches to conform to the world rather than to transform the world. One evidence of this is the tendency to measure the success of churches in worldly, material terms. We talk entirely too much about the size of budgets and the cost of buildings. The materialistic spirit threatens to capture our churches.

Even some church and denominational leaders seem to be more concerned about our prestige in the world than in our power to change the world. This is a contributor to some of our problems, such as the tendency to build and to maintain too many and too elaborate institutions.

Third, there is an apparent tendency to resist change in a rapidly changing world. On the surface, this may sound contradictory to the preceding. We will see, however, that it is not contradictory when we understand that the major movements of change come up from the masses. These movements are usually resisted by the privileged.

Many, and possibly most, members of the better established churches and denominations tend to identify with the status quo. Entirely too many of us have failed to understand that the old ways of life are on the way out.

Fourth, there is a tendency to stress quantity more than quality. There is a need for both, but we need desperately more emphasis on quality in local churches, in denominations, and in denominational institutions and agencies. We cannot indefinitely have the quantity without improving the quality. This is true of evangelistic results and of the work of our churches and denominations in general.

Fifth, there is a tendency toward a controlled press. This may be an accomplished fact rather than a tendency. It is, potentially, extremely dangerous. Church papers are usually owned and controlled by some denominational group or agency. Most of them cannot live without denominational support.

We should help the editors of such papers to maintain as much independence as possible. We should also be grateful for courageous editors, who speak as prophets of God through the pages of their papers. Let us not forget, however, that a press controlled by any church or denominational entity is a threat to our churches and denominations.

# 39. Evangelism and Social Concern

CHRISTIANS are beginning to see with increasing clarity that they need not and must not choose between evangelism and social concern. The decision must be both/and rather than either/or.

Some of us may function primarily in the area of evangelism. Others may operate primarily in the area of applied Christianity or social compassion and concern. Let all of us have respect for one another and for our distinctive contributions to the cause of Christ and to the work of our churches.

It should not be difficult for Christians to recognize that evangelism and social concern or ethics belong together. They were joined together in the life and ministry of Jesus. He came to seek and to save that which was lost. He also went about doing good, ministering to the needs of people. He not only said, "Go . . . make disciples," he also said, "teach them to obey everything that I have commanded you."

A proper understanding of evangelism will indicate that it is much more inclusive than many of us have realized. Through evangelism the total person is brought into a vital, life-changing union with the resurrected Christ. We do not "win souls" to the Lord. We win people to faith in and commitment to the Lord. When properly interpreted this relationship to the risen Lord inevitably affects every area of our lives.

In the contemporary world it is possible that many people will not respond to the preaching of the gospel if we are unconcerned about their daily lives and problems. The responsibility for such concern rests on individual church members as well as on churches and pastors. If we were more concerned about people as neighbors and friends, we doubtless would have more of them to attend the services of our churches and more of them would respond to the preaching of the gospel.

We can sum up the matter by saying that our social concern

103

will not be on a sound basis unless it stems from a heart that yearns for men and women to open their hearts and lives to Christ as Savior and Lord. On the other hand, our evangelism will be increasingly unproductive unless it is accompanied by a genuine compassion for people as people, along with a sincere desire to share their problems and to minister to their needs.

May the good Lord help us to keep evangelism and social concern vibrant and vital and in proper balance in the life and work of our churches and denominations.

# 40. Neglected Aspects of Stewardship

THERE ARE SOME phases of stewardship that are neglected, at least to some degree, by most churches. The emphasis tends to be too exclusively upon money and material possessions.

One neglected aspect of stewardship is the steward himself. The steward as a child of God does not belong to himself; he has been bought with a price (1 Cor. 6:19-20). He belongs to and is responsible unto God. Once he is gripped by this conception of his relationship to God, there will be present in his life the foundation for real and abiding stewardship. He will see, as every child of God ought to see, that since he belongs to God everything that he has also belongs to God.

The steward is not only to be faithful in the giving of tithes and offerings, he is also to recognize that the nine-tenths as well as the one-tenth belongs to God.

Since the Christian belongs to God, he will recognize that he is responsible to God not only for how much he gives and how he uses his money but also for the way he makes his money.

He will also understand that Christian stewardship is more inclusive than money and material possessions. The steward is the trustee of his total personality. His influence and even his attitudes are included in his stewardship. Christian stewardship is as broad as life itself.

Another aspect of stewardship that is frequently overlooked or neglected is the stewardship of the group. Not only is the individual a steward or trustee, but the family, the church, the community, the nation, the denomination, and even a civilization are stewards. For example, our churches and our denominational agencies and institutions are stewards of the monies that come into their treasuries. They, with their leaders, should have a deep sense of responsibility for what they do with what has been given to the Lord and dedicated to his purposes in the world.

It possibly should be added that the stewardship responsibility of the church and the denomination has a two-directional look: it looks to the people who support them but primarily to the Lord who is the owner of all.

Another aspect of stewardship that is often overlooked is the stewardship of things spiritual. This quality of stewardship along with a proper emphasis on the steward provide the soundest basis for an effective stewardship program. It was Peter who said, "As every man hath received the gift, even so minister the same one to another, as good stewards of the manifold grace of God" (1 Peter 4:10, KJV), or as Phillips puts it, the "magnificently varied grace of God."

We are stewards or trustees of the grace of God that has saved and also sustained and blessed us through the years. The greater the blessings, the greater our responsibility to share them with others.

The "magnificently varied grace" of God has not only been revealed in our lives but also in the Bible. The grace that is revealed in the latter is sufficient for the salvation of all men who will open their hearts to the resurrected Christ. As children of God we are stewards of that grace. We are to share it with the peoples of the world.

Likewise, the basic stewardship of the church and the denomination is the stewardship of things spiritual. Churches are to share the gospel with the people of the local community and with the peoples of all the world.

What a difference it would make in our giving as individuals and in our sharing as churches if we were possessed with a deep conviction that our basic stewardship is a stewardship of the grace of God. We would readily see that money, which is material, can be used to achieve spiritual ends.

Giving and sharing would become glorious as we recognize that all of us are laborers together with the Lord in his work in the local community and to the ends of the earth. There would be a thrill to giving that otherwise it lacks.

# 41. Democracy and Dictatorship

THERE IS ALWAYS a possibility that a dictatorship will arise out of a democracy, whether political or religious. One factor is the presence in the democracy of some people with an inflated opinion of their capacity to lead or rule. Their desire for power may be purely selfish, or they may seek a place of power to enable them to achieve what they consider to be best for the people.

Another reason that a dictatorship may evolve from a democracy is the unwillingness of many people to accept the responsibilities of decision-making and self-government. They will surrender the liberties that a democracy provides in order to avoid the responsibilities that those liberties entail.

Both of the above factors may be at work in a religious as well as in a political democracy. For example, members of a church may permit or even insist that the pastor, the staff, the deacons, or the committees make decisions. When they do this they are providing the basis for the rise of a dictatorship, individual or group.

When recommendations are automatically approved, the democratic process, preserved in form but not in substance, is being used to destroy democracy itself. This is particularly true if questions are frowned upon, and if those who disagree are considered uncooperative, if not actually heretical. The larger the church the greater is the danger ordinarily that this attitude will develop and predominate.

If democracy is lost in a church, a major factor will be that most church members have abdicated their responsibility. A vacuum is created, and vacuums do not remain unoccupied very long. There are usually individuals or small groups that are ready to move in as people in general move out. This means, among other things, that in any church that has a pastor, a deacon, or someone else who is a dictator, the church must share the responsibility for the rise of the dictatorship. This is just as true of dictatorship by a group as by an individual.

Some who become dictators, and many people in general, fail to make a proper distinction between dictatorship and positive leadership. One can exercise the latter without being a dictator. The line of distinction may be rather fine or narrow, but it is very important.

A pastor cannot provide the leadership that a church needs unless he is positive in his leadership. But he should not be a dictator. He should know the direction in which he believes the Lord wants the church to move. He also should know and suggest ways to attain the goals he has for the church, but he should never seek to force his ideas on the church. He should involve others in refining and defining goals and strategies. When he does this he is strengthening democracy in the church.

If the pastor is a positive leader rather than a dictator, he will not be offended if some member or members of the church disagree with him. He will not consider such a difference an affront to his leadership.

Let all of us in any place of leadership, whether pastors, deacons, teachers, carefully walk the narrow dividing line between positive leadership and dictatorship. Our ability to do so will be an important factor in determining the effectiveness of our leadership and the preservation of democracy. This is just as true in the denomination as it is in the local church.

# ● VIII.
# THE DISINHERITED

# 42. Race
## and the Nature of the Church

THE NATURE of the church creates for it some very real problems and yet some tremendous potentialities in the area of race. The church is a divine-human institution.

Its human nature is evident in the fact that it cannot help but be influenced by its environment. It is always located in a human situation. It cannot totally ignore or detach itself completely from its culture. To do so would mean that it would not be able to minister effectively to the culture.

Also, the church is a human institution in the sense that it is composed of men and women. Those men and women are immature and imperfect. If the church is to minister effectively to them, it must begin where they are and seek to lead them to where they ought to be. This is just as true in the area of race as anywhere else.

It is most unfortunate, however, if any church fails to recognize and to respond to its divine nature. It ministers to men and women in a particular cultural situation, but it ministers to them in the name of the Lord. It gets its commission from the Lord. Its basic purpose is to promote the cause of Christ, the kingdom of God among men.

Also, the message that the church teaches in the classroom and preaches from the pulpit is of divine origin. It is the Word of God addressed to men. How unfortunate if that message on race or on any other issue is trimmed or toned down to fit the particular human situation.

As a result of its divine-human nature there tends to be a continuing tension within the church. If that tension is not there, then the dual nature of the church is not being kept in proper focus. This tension in recent years in many churches has been more evident regarding race than in any other area. It should be remem-

bered that there is no real hope for the movement of the church toward God's ideal for it without such tension.

There is a continuing temptation to excuse the church's limitations or imperfections on the basis of its human nature. Many churches clearly violate the Christian spirit in the area of human relations in general and race relations in particular. But the claim is made that the churches cannot do otherwise or they will lose the opportunity to minister to the spiritual needs of people.

But what about the divine nature of the church? Can any church properly claim to be the "church of God" or claim to have Christ as its head and yet fail not only to proclaim the Word of God on human relations but also to practice that Word in its own fellowship?

It may not greatly damage the church and the cause of Christ if a church considers it impossible for it to "go all the way" in the area of race relations at a particular place and at a particular time. It will do irreparable harm, however, to the church and to the cause for a church to contend that its very imperfect expression of its divine nature is God's ultimate will for the church in the area of race.

There is no hope for advance toward God's ideal for our churches unless there is maintained a constant tension between where those churches are now and where by his grace they should be.

Churches can never lift the world toward God's ideal unless there is maintained a wholesome tension between what they teach, preach, and practice and what the world believes and does. There is no area in which this is more true than in the area of race.

# 43. Churches and Race Relations

IT IS TIME for white Christians to take some giant steps forward in their attitudes toward, relations to, and work with Negroes. Entirely too many churches, as well as individuals, have been satisfied merely to give a little material aid.

What can be done on the local church level? We can seek to maintain or restore lost lines of communication. White pastors and Negro pastors can have fellowship together in prayer and study. Groups of young people, women, men, and others can exchange programs. Pulpits can be exchanged. Special music can be provided.

Churches should open their doors to people of all classes and races. Some have done this, many more should. How can any church claim to be the church where Christ is head if it does not open its doors for worship to all and its membership to all men and women of "like faith and order" regardless of color or culture?

When we open our doors we may discover that few, if any, Negro Christians want to be members of our white churches. Most who will come at first will be college students. They are in colleges and universities with young white people. It is more or less natural that some of them will want to attend church with friends they have made on the campus.

Although it seems for the indefinite future that comparatively few Negroes will want to be members of white churches, they do want the doors open. They want every phase of our predominantly white society available to them. Would not we, who are white, want the same thing if we belonged to a minority group and if we were excluded from any aspect of the society in which we lived? We would have knocked harder and more persistently on those doors than they have.

Let us not forget, however, that churches may desegregate without real integration. The latter will not occur until Negroes and those of other minority groups are accepted into the life of the church on the same basis as white members. They must be utilized in places of leadership on the basis of their ability, training, and spiritual maturity. Most churches that have Negro members, and there are a considerable number, have not progressed very far in integrating them into the life and structures of the church.

Churches, however, will be moving in the right direction if they recognize the need for an open-door policy regarding peoples of all classes and colors. If they will open their doors, and if their members will open their minds and hearts, then Negro neighbors and friends will determine how much desegregation and integration there will be in our churches.

# 44. Paternalism Versus Fraternalism

DR. ALLIX B. JAMES, vice-president and dean of the School of Theology of Virginia Union University recently spoke to the Evangelistic Conference of the Virginia Baptist Convention. It would help Southern Baptists and other church and denominational groups to move in the right direction in race relations if their leaders would ask capable Negroes, such as Dr. James, to speak frankly to their meetings about what white Christians and churches can do to improve their relations with Negro Christians and black people in general.

Toward the close of his address, Dr. James spoke concerning "white" attitudes that are most objectionable to Negroes. No attempt will be made to set forth all of these. I want to concentrate on one particular attitude that is the source of other attitudes that are objectionable. Dr. James himself said that heading the list was "the old traditional pattern of 'paternalism.'" He further said that the master-slave, superior-inferior perspectives must disappear entirely.

Furthermore, whites must get away from the "dole" system, whether it is money or service, and whether or not the "dole" is handed out by individual "white" Christians, by a church, or by a denominational agency. The "dole" may be accepted and yet the gap between white and Negro Christians may be widened.

We are beyond the time, if there ever was such a time, when the paternalistic approach will be effective. Fraternalism must be substituted. Paternalism stems from a sense of superiority. Fraternalism is a product of a deep sense of oneness in Christ. Regardless of culture or color, we have come into the family of God through the same door, the door of faith. Also, our heavenly Father is no respecter of persons. He looks on the heart and not on the color of the skin. All of us, white and black, should seek to be like our Father in our attitudes toward one another.

There also needs to be a proper understanding of "fraternalism." Negroes must be accepted and treated as equals, not as younger or less mature brothers. Some may be immature, but many of them are more mature intellectually, morally, and spiritually than many white people. We must avoid the stereotyping of Negroes, just as we do not want them to stereotype us.

Once a pattern, such as paternalism, is established it is difficult to change it. Even when we try to treat Negroes as brothers, we tend to have a paternalistic hangover. Local churches too frequently put on "Bible schools for Negro churches" rather than offer to be of help if they can. Many churches should have integrated schools with an integrated faculty as well as both Negro and white children.

Churches and church bodies and agencies frequently plan meetings, such as evangelistic conferences and campaigns, and then invite Negro churches and church leaders to cooperate. If we expect them to participate, let us invite them to share in the planning.

Let us move from paternalism to fraternalism or brotherhood.

# 45. Ghettos: Past and Present

THERE HAS BEEN in recent years a great deal of discussion of the ghettos. Originally, "ghetto" referred to the area of the city where Jews were required to live. When I was a college student there was considerable interest in the ghettos in the larger industrial areas of the North and East. These were, in the main, Irish, Italian, and Polish ghettos. In addition, there were in a few cities, such as New York and San Francisco, some unusually sharply isolated Chinese ghettos. People who lived in these and other ghettos were separated in most ways from the mainstream of American life. They maintained to a large degree their distinctive customs and culture.

Until quite recently there was a considerable period of time when little was heard concerning the ghettos. One could still visit Chinatown in some of our larger cities. But the other ghettos had largely disappeared. The second and third generation children of European immigrants moved culturally and in many cases actually or physically from the ghettos. They became Americans rather than Irish-Americans, Italian-Americans, or Polish-Americans. Chinese and other Orientals found this movement to be more difficult but not impossible.

The contemporary ghetto is quite different from the ghettos of the past. The vast majority of the residents of the present-day ghettos are not immigrants from Europe or the Orient. Most of them have migrated to the urban centers from the rural areas of the South. Furthermore, ghettos are far more prevalent than formerly in smaller cities. In other words, the ghetto is a more common phenomenon in the contemporary period.

Also, contemporary Negro ghettos generally lack the inner cohesion and strength found in some of the former immigrant ghettos. The residents of the latter had their roots firmly fixed in a historic culture from which they had come. Many Negroes do not identify with any culture. Their rootlessness is a major factor

120

in their frustration. This is particularly true of the poorer Negroes in the ghettos of the urban centers who do not feel that they have become an integral part of American life.

In contrast to the residents of the earlier ghettos, the Negroes have the handicap of color. This, in a racially conscious society, makes it much more difficult for children and grandchildren to move from the ghettos. Many find themselves trapped.

One thing that increases the pressure in the contemporary ghetto is the fact that those who live there, particularly the young, have caught a glimpse of the American creed or dream. They have a deepening desire that the dream become a reality for them, and they have developed a strong discontent with a ghetto type of existence.

When the pressure is strong against their moving up and out of the ghetto, it is more or less natural that the residents of the ghetto will react in one of two ways. They will either use drastic means if need be in an attempt to break down the wall that separates them from full participation in the American way of life, or they will seek to build within the ghetto a separate and distinctly Negro community.

There is some evidence of the latter in the contemporary period, although evidently the majority of Negroes still prefer and hope for a thorough integration of the Negro people into American life.

## 46. Poor: Past and Present

I GREW UP in a home of poverty. My father was in turn a farm laborer, a section hand on a railroad, and a sharecropper, although we were not acquainted with the term "sharecropper."

We were poor but my dad, typical of an East Tennessee hillbilly, was radically independent. He believed that a man should stand on his own feet and work out his own problems. He would not have thought of accepting aid from anyone or from any agency.

He and Mother planted in our minds the idea that poverty did not have to be a permanent handicap. They inspired us to believe that we could move up and out of it. They also insisted that while we did not have much we would be good stewards of what we had. The tithe box sat on the mantle above the fireplace. Also, Mother frequently said: "We may not have much, but we can keep what we have clean." And she did.

Like some of you, my experience has made it difficult for me to understand today's poor. Some of us need to recognize that there are some important differences in the poor of the past and the present.

When Dad was a section hand we lived in a small town. It was easy then for boys who wanted to work to find employment. I started when I was ten years old working before and after school, on Saturday, and during the summer months. From that time on I paid for my own clothes. Also, we had a big garden that provided more than enough vegetables for the family.

When we became sharecroppers, we had a rent-free house in which to live. We not only had a garden but also chickens, hogs, and a couple of cows. We had much of our living from the farm. Mother also sold eggs, milk, and butter. We did not always have a balanced diet, but we had enough to eat most of the time.

In contrast, many of the poor in the contemporary period are crowded into the ghettos of our larger cities. Rent has to be paid.

All the food for the family has to be brought in from the outside. Frequently the father does not have the skills to compete in an increasingly technical society. If he has work, his income is inadequate to meet the mounting costs of housing, clothing, and feeding a family in an urban area.

Furthermore, relatively few even of the teen-age children can find any type of employment. Many of them develop an attitude of hopelessness. They see little if any chance for them to improve their status. Poverty tends to become a way of life for them and in turn for their children.

Most of the contemporary poor have grown up in a time when more and more people have looked to the government to solve their problems. This has not only been true of the poor, it has tended to be true of the farmers, laborers, businessmen, and people in general. In our complex society this dependence may be more or less necessary, but it has weakened the desire and the determination of many people to do what they can to solve their own problems.

The preceding statement should not be interpreted as blaming the poor for their situation. Rather, it is an attempt to point out that the poor of the present, to a considerable degree, are victims of the system.

# 47. Poverty: More Than Money

Local, state, and federal governments can pour billions of dollars into the antipoverty program and yet not solve the problem. Any effective approach to the problem and particularly any permanent solution requires more than money.

This is not an appeal for less money. There is entirely too much complaint by some people about the amount that is being spent to relieve some of the problems of the poor.

A recent article in the *New York Times* said that Americans would spend more than $700 million a year to purchase dogs and puppies. Less than half that amount goes into the Job Corps and only approximately $630 million into all the Community Action Programs. The story also said that an additional $450 million would be spent by the American people just for accessories for dogs—collars, leashes, etc. This will be more than the annual cost for the Headstart program.

Certainly we should not complain about the amount of money being spent in the antipoverty effort. We may properly raise some questions about how efficiently it is being used.

We do believe, however, that money alone will not and cannot solve a problem that is moral as well as material. Many who work with the poor and many of the poor themselves recognize that something in addition to money is needed.

One thing that is tremendously important is the desire, the move, or the drive to come up out of poverty. To accept dependence on others as something that is permanent impoverishes the soul and the character of the poor. Some way there must be aroused within them a deep hunger to help themselves, to stand on their own feet, to contribute in a worthy way to the solution of their own problems.

This is where the family, the school, and the church can make a significant contribution. For example, churches may have some

responsibility to provide for the material needs of the poor, but their greatest contribution will be the creation within the poor and particularly within the maturing children of the poor the inner urge or drive to help themselves. The church can also cultivate within them the faith to believe that the Lord will strengthen them as they seek to surmount their environment.

The preceding will not be easy for a church in the ghetto or in a pocket of poverty. Some way, however, the leadership of those churches must inspire the churches to become islands of hope. If the churches succeed in doing this, they can be instruments of God in lifting the community itself to a higher level of living, to a spirit of genuine self-help.

And let parents also remember that even in the most impoverished circumstances they still have a responsibility to build character into their sons and daughters. They can do this by what they say, but even more important they can do it by the kind of lives they live.

# IX.
# CITIZENSHIP

# 48. Law, Order, and Justice

OUR DEMOCRATIC way of life cannot be preserved without respect both for law and for those who enact, interpret, and enforce the law. Just as surely, a democracy cannot permanently survive unless it provides justice for its citizens. For a democracy to remain healthy, these two, law and order on the one hand and justice on the other, must be kept in proper balance. They must move along together.

In contemporary America there has been a breakdown to a distressing degree of law and order. This in turn has stemmed to a considerable degree from the struggle for justice by many of our citizens.

Extremists at both ends of the present struggle over civil rights have contributed to the breakdown of respect for law and for those who interpret and enforce the law. Some of those who now cry the loudest for "law and order" are the very ones who sought in every possible way, a few years ago, to evade compliance with the courts' decisions regarding desegregation. They were and some still are particularly harsh in their criticisms of the United States Supreme Court. Some have even accused the Court of following the Communist line. Such contributes to a breakdown not only of respect for the Court but also of law in general.

Let us repeat that both order and justice are essential for a healthy social order. Unfortunately, some who seek to attain justice use methods that tend to undermine respect for law and order. When this is done the cause of justice is ultimately hurt rather than helped.

On the other hand, some people would maintain law and order even if it meant the denial of justice to some of our citizens. Ultimately this is self-defeating. The law will not be respected by those who cannot find justice under it, and order ultimately will be undermined.

The relative importance of order and justice are determined by

the situation. In a time of rapid change and revolution, such as the contemporary period, justice should be given primacy. This can be done without a reckless abandonment of law and order.

Let anyone who believes he is justified in disobeying a particular law seek to do so in such a way as not to lose respect or to cause others to lose respect for law as such and for those who enforce it. On the other hand, let the majority who have the power be sure that they are just as concerned about justice as they are about law and order. If they are not, the law and order that they may now have will not be on a sound basis. It will at best be uncertain and unstable.

It should not take a wise man to see the relevance of the preceding to both whites and blacks in the present racial crisis in the United States.

# 49. The Bible and Civil Disobedience

WHAT SHOULD BE the attitude of Christians toward civil disobedience? Should they approve or disapprove, or should theirs be a selective approval or disapproval? By "selective" we mean selective on the basis of causes, methods, and spirit.

Some people have made an effort to bring the Bible into the present controversy concerning civil disobedience. For example, some contend that Jesus was a revolutionary and that Paul disobeyed the civil authorities. On the other hand, some would use Romans 13:1 and other Scriptures to insist that civil disobedience is always wrong.

Whether or not it is correct to consider Jesus a revolutionary depends on the meaning attached to the word. His teachings unquestionably were and still are revolutionary. Nothing would produce a more drastic revolution in our world than for those who claim to be followers of Christ to take seriously his teachings and seek to apply them in their lives and to the life of the world.

If by "revolutionary" it is meant that Jesus attempted to overthrow constituted authority, then we would have to conclude that he was not a revolutionary.

Also, it should be remembered, although it may not be particularly significant, that the disobedience of Jesus was against religious rather than political authorities. And even in this area his "rebellion" was not against the faith but against the misinterpretation of that faith.

The followers of Jesus, according to Acts, found it necessary at times to disobey the civil as well as the religious authorities. The position of the early Christians was stated by Peter and John when they said that they had to obey God rather than man.

The preceding means, among other things, that disobedience, from the biblical perspective, can be justified under some conditions. We know, for example, that Paul was imprisoned because of

131

his disobedience. The only specific cause for disobedience that is clearly evident in the Scriptures is the authorities' forbidding the disciples to preach. Of course, we should not forget the statement of the general principle that the child of God must obey God rather than man. This might mean disobedience for various reasons.

It seems clear from the biblical perspective that any disobedience by Christians should be done regretfully. Also, it should be in such a way as not to undermine respect for constituted authority. This means, among other things, that the right of the state to punish will be recognized, as well as the right of the individual to disobey. This in turn means that there will be no attempt to overthrow the constituted authority.

If these concepts are applied to contemporary civil disobedience, what must be our own conclusions?

First, we cannot deny the right of nonviolent civil disobedience. On the other hand, we must conclude that much contemporary civil disobedience would have to be disapproved. This disapproval would be based primarily on the motive and particularly the spirit of the disobedience.

Each civil disobedience incident or movement would have to be judged on its own merits.

# 50. Independent or Party Man?

ON ELECTION DAY will you vote a straight party ticket, or is there at least a possibility that you will split your vote? Whatever your answer to this question may be, it is hoped that you will vote.

Admittedly, it is difficult if not impossible for some men, particularly politicians, to be nonparty men. Also, more Christian men and women should be active in precinct, county, and state political affairs; and such individuals have to identify themselves with a particular party. This does not mean, however, that they should never cross over party lines. After all, the good of the country and the purposes of God should be considered more important for the Christian than loyalty to a party.

My personal opinion is that the vast majority of Christians should be politically independent. In this way, they can let the man running for office or the issues rather than the party label determine how they vote.

Also, by being an independent, they can best make their influence felt in the political world. Independent voters determine the outcome of most elections. Because independent voters are so determinative in elections, they are the main hope for a clean-up when the party in power gets corrupt.

Another reason for being independent in politics is that there is not much to choose between the parties. Both major parties have conservative and liberal wings. The only difference is a difference of degree. Both parties, in a sense and to a degree, are split personalities. Even party platforms are strikingly similar on many issues. There would be a sounder basis for faithful adherence to one party if there could be a poltical realignment with a clear-cut distinction between a conservative and a liberal party.

An additional reason for my political independence is a personal aversion for most labels, particularly theological and political ones. This aversion is especially strong for a self-imposed label. When a

133

person voluntarily accepts a label he tends to limit himself in his search for truth. The only restraint that a child of God should want should be the restraint of truth itself.

The Christian's vote is a part of his stewardship responsibility. How he votes is his business but it should be an expression of his supreme loyalty to God rather than to any human institution or organization. I personally believe that ordinarily the independent voter rather than the party man can more clearly demonstrate such loyalty. An additional word should be said: We should never permit differences in politics to become a test of fellowship with other Christians.

# 51. One-Issue Voters

ONE OF THE MOST common mistakes of many Christian citizens is that they are one-issue voters. If a politician is right, from their perspective on that particular issue, they will vote for him. Frequently they will do this, regardless of how much or how little background he has for the responsibilities of the office he seeks.

The one issue will most frequently be something in the area of personal morality. For example, if the one seeking an office does not drink, many Christians will vote for him regardless of what else he may or may not do, and regardless of his position on the major issues of the race. On the other hand, if he has been divorced, many will not vote for him, although by training and experience he may be the best-qualified man seeking that particular office. For some Christian citizens a candidate's religious affiliation will determine whether or not they will vote for him.

On the basis of personal morality and religion affiliation, there may not be a real choice between the candidates. In that case, some of us will center on one particular social or political issue. The position of the candidates on that issue will be the major factor in determining the one for whom we will vote.

The issue may be something the candidate is for or something he is against, and too frequently it is the latter. We feel so strongly about that particular matter that we tend to vote for the one who most fully agrees with our position. The issue may be "crime on the streets," "foreign aid," "liquor by the drink," "parimutuel betting," "the political machine," "urban renewal," "war and peace," or some other favorite subject of ours. Whatever the issue, it may have become such an obsession with us that we let it determine too exclusively how we vote.

I am not suggesting that any of the issues mentioned are of minor importance. For example, a Christian certainly should give serious consideration to the personal morality of candidates. He may wisely give some consideration to their religious affiliation. He should seek

to know the position of candidates regarding all the issues that he personally thinks are important.

What I am attempting to emphasize is that we should not become so enamored with one particular issue that we fail to give proper consideration to other issues that may be of equal importance. Also, it will be wise for us to seek to determine whether or not the candidate's position on an issue represents his honest personal conviction or is a political convenience.

One candidate announced that his platform was the Ten Commandments and the Sermon on the Mount. It would be unfortunate if Christian men and women "fell" for this kind of propaganda. At least, they should ask how he would apply the Ten Commandments and the Sermon on the Mount to the daily problems that he would face if elected.

There are at least three things that Christian citizens should consider in determining the one for whom they will vote: (1) The basic character and integrity, as best they can be determined, of the candidates. (2) The position of the candidates on all the issues that are revelant to the office they are seeking. (3) The ability, the training, and the experience of the candidates to fulfill the responsibilities of the office.

# 52. The Christian and War

WAR THROUGH the centuries has been a continuing and a perplexing problem for many Christians. It has been particularly difficult for some when they have had to make a personal decision concerning their active participation in war. Four or five more or less distinct positions have developed. Some Christians contend that war is exclusively the responsibility of the government. If one's country is at war, the citizen's total responsibility is obedience to the commands of his nation. Some even suggest that the nation and not the individual citizen is responsible for those he may kill in times of war.

Also, there are some Christians who have no personal difficulty about full participation in war. They see no necessary conflict between their Christian faith and active participation. They are sometimes referred to as "conscientious participants."

There are still others who consider war under some conditions the lesser of two evils. They say that since we are evil and the world in which we live is evil, many decisions are not between an unmixed good and an unmixed evil, not between white and black. Rather, many decisions are in the gray area. The best a Christian can do under such conditions is to choose the lesser of two evils. Some insist that the Christian's decision regarding war in general and his participation in war is frequently if not usually such a decision. Some evil is involved whatever he does. He should seek to follow the course that will entail the maximum of good and the minimum of evil.

Then, there have been some Christians through the centuries who have said that they could not in good conscience participate in war. These are the pacifists or conscientious objectors. There is more than one type of these. Some are limited conscientious objectors. They are the ones who admit that they cannot completely avoid involvement in the sins of an evil world, including war. They do contend, however, that they must limit the extent of their involvement if they are to maintain their own personal integrity. Most limited conscientious objectors will accept noncombatant service such as the medical corps. They will participate in war up to the point of taking human life.

There have been some Christians, particularly in the first two Christian centuries and in more recent years, who are unlimited conscientious objectors. They are the absolutists or perfectionists. They say that they cannot and will not have anything to do with the whole war system. They are the ones in the United States who have gone to prison or to conscientious objector camps rather than serve with the armed forces.

Each Christian, regardless of his personal position concerning war, should defend and respect the right of conscience of every other Christian. Regardless of how much Christians may differ concerning one's participation in war, we should never permit our differences to damage or disrupt our fellowship with one another.

Let us beware of developing a self-righteous attitude concerning our particular position. There may be men and women who are better Christians than we are who take a drastically different position regarding the Christian and war.

# 53. The Selective
# Conscientious Objector

THERE HAS ARISEN in the contemporary period a new type of conscientious objector. The federal government and many churches have not decided what to do about him.

There were some conscientious objectors during World War I and a noticeable increase during World War II. These, in the main, were objectors to war in general. Our national government more or less uniformly respected the rights of conscience of such objectors. They were permitted to become medics or enter some other type of noncombatant service. If they were limitless objectors the government provided conscientious objectors camps for them, although the objectors had to arrange for their own support.

Now, however, there are some young people who are not necessarily objectors to war in general but to a particular war, such as the Vietnam conflict. These selective conscientious objectors have created some problems for the federal government. The existing draft law provides for conscientious objection against war as such but not for the objector to a particular war. Furthermore, only the religiously motivated conscientious objector is provided for. Some of the contemporary objectors base their objections on philosophical or political grounds.

The preceding helps to explain but it does not excuse some of the extreme methods that have been used by some contemporary objectors and their supporters.

One of the continuing problems of draft boards as well as military personnel is to determine when an individual is really a conscientious objector and when he is simply seeking to avoid military service. It is particularly difficult for the authorities when the young person does not belong to one of the historic peace churches.

What is and what should be the attitude of the non-peace churches toward the conscientious objector in their own fellowship and in general? It is possible that there are very few, if any, such

139

objectors in most of our churches. However, if our churches are consistent in the application of our concept of the right of individual conscience, then they will defend the right of the conscientious objector, selective or otherwise.

The only question our churches and church leaders should ask about the conscientious objector is whether or not he has carefully thought through and is honest in his position. Protestants in general contend that the right of conscience of the individual person should be respected. This should be just as true regarding war as it is regarding worship or anything else.

A local church with 200 or 2,000 members might have one lone conscientious objector in its fellowship. The 199 or the 1,999 other members should defend the right of conscience of that one member. They should surround him with understanding and Christian love.

A denomination may have 1,000,000 or 10,000,000 members. There might be only one sincere selective conscientious objector in the whole denomination. My viewpoint is and has been for many years that the other 999,999 or 9,999,999 should defend the right of the one conscientious objector. To do less is to violate something that is basic in our Protestant way of life. If it should be necessary for the conscientious objector to go to a conscientious objector camp and to provide his own financial support, his local church and/or his denomination should provide such support for him.

On the other hand, the conscientious objector should scrupulously avoid any sense of superiority. He should respect just as much the position of those who disagree with him as he expects them to respect and defend him in his position.

# ● X.
# CONCLUDING CONVICTIONS

# 54. Compromise
## and the Democratic Process

"COMPROMISE" is considered a nasty word by some people. They contend that it reveals a lack of conviction, courage, and character.

Compromise may be a nasty word, but it is necessary in the operation of a democracy in church or state. Most decisions that are made through the democratic process require some compromise.

"Politics" has been defined as the art of the possible. This definition applies in particular and primarily to a democracy. Our churches and church organizations are not political entities, but some of the methods and techniques that are integral to political democracy are applicable in varying degrees to them.

Decisions, as in a political democracy, are arrived at through discussion and conference. An essential phase of such decision-making is the art of compromise—and it is an art.

Many times in a democracy, political or religious, no decision can or will be reached without some compromise. An individual or a group, small or large, that is unwilling to compromise or make adjustments will frequently unnecessarily slow down the decision-making process or even make a decision impossible.

An unwillingness to compromise may also disrupt or destroy the fellowship in a group. On the other hand, if the fellowship in the church or religious group is to be maintained on the highest level, all of the compromise or adjustment must not be made by one individual or by those representing one particular position. There must be a willingness on the part of all "to give a little in order to gain a little."

Compromise does not do any serious damage to the integrity of an individual or a group so long as the end attained is greater or more significant than the sacrifice that was made. This is particularly true when the end could not have been attained without the compromise.

For compromise to be most effective and least damaging there must be enough maturity by the individual or the group to distinguish between the essential and the nonessential. There can properly be more of a readiness to compromise on the latter than on the former. There are limits to how far an individual or a group can go in compromising on essentials and still maintain integrity.

There may come a time, for example, when the individual will have to take a stand even if he has to stand alone. When he reaches the limits of his accommodation, if the majority votes against him he should accept the decision graciously. He should beware of a martyr complex, of a self-righteous spirit, or of an attitude of superior enlightenment. After all, there is at least a possibility that he may be wrong. He should react in such a way as to strengthen rather than to weaken the fellowship of the group. He should trust the future for his vindication.

# 55. Democracy and Its Creative Minority

BASIC IN DEMOCRACY, political or religious, is majority rule accompanied with respect for the rights of the minority. The latter involves the right to attempt through peaceful means to change the viewpoint or opinion of the majority.

There is one minority group that has a rough time in a democracy. It is the creative minority. This implies that not all minorities are creative and also that only a minority of people in a democracy are creative. The majority of people prefer not to be disturbed. They may be critical of things as they are, but most of them are traditionalists and defenders of the status quo.

The strong desire for stability that seems to be characteristic of a democracy is one reason why the creative minority has a hard time in a democracy. By "creative minority" we are not thinking primarily of an organized group but rather of individuals. Frequently there is a tendency in a democracy to ostracize such individuals.

There also seems to be built into the democratic process a tendency toward the leveling of people. When one rises very far above the ordinary level the tendency is to push him back down. This tendency is particularly strong when he rises above the ordinary level in ideas and ideals, in motives and purposes, in dreams and thought.

The leadership of a democracy and the majority who support that leadership evidently feel threatened by creative minds and souls, who challenge the old ways and are willing to try the new. Creative individuals are disturbers of the status quo, and from the perspective of the majority, there are few sins that are more serious.

There is a tendency at times in a religious democracy to apply a particular theological label to its creative minority. Because they are open to new insights and new strategies they are frequently considered "liberal." They may, however, be basically conserva-

145

tive in their theology while being liberal in regard to structures and programs.

A creative minority is needed in any democracy. Otherwise the democracy will tend to become static, and will lose its relevance in a rapidly changing world. The creative minority may be like a thorn in the flesh at times, but it is needed to suggest new insights and new directions.

There should never be a tendency to label one as "an obstructionist," "a nonconformist," or "a liberal" simply because he suggests a different perspective or procedure.

It is tremendously important, if a democracy is to remain healthy and dynamic, for the right to differ in love to be recognized and respected. We should be very careful about reading or forcing anyone out of the church or denomination because he disagrees with the majority and/or with the leadership. There is a possibility that a minority perspective may represent the wave of the future. A minority may be pointing the way in which God would have us to go.

At the same time, the minority, if it is to be really creative, must respect the majority and seek to work within the existing structures to bring about the desired changes.

## 56. Freedom and Maturity

ONE OF THE MAJOR handicaps of our churches is the immaturity of so many church members. There are entirely too many who are mature in years and yet babes in Christ. They ought to be teachers of others but still need to be taught the first principles of our faith.

One reason for the immaturity of many Christians is their failure to appropriate the freedom there is in Christ. Also, they frequently fail to understand the relation of freedom and maturity.

There is no maturity without freedom and the responsibility that freedom brings. Parents know that this is true. One of their most delicate and difficult tasks is to know when to shift decision-making from themselves to their children. It may be tragic if freedom is given to the child prematurely, but it can also be tragic if it is postponed too late. One matures as he handles freedom responsibly.

What is true of the child in the home is also true of the child of God. He must have freedom if he is to mature. The latter is true of the preacher in the pulpit and of the layman in the pew, of the teacher on the platform and the pupil at the desk, of the scholar who writes and of the one who reads what he writes.

It may be that churches suffer from a shortage of prophetic leadership because of a lack of freedom to differ.

It is also possible that some Christian groups have not contributed as much as they should have in the area of scholarship because they have failed to provide adequately the atmosphere and spirit that are essential for a creatively mature scholarship.

As one matures he will have a clearer insight into the distinction between essential or basic freedom and freedom regarding the nonessentials.

The maturing Christian will increasingly understand that basic freedom, other than freedom from the enslavement of sin, involves at least two closely related concepts or ideas: (1) freedom of access to God, (2) freedom to do the will of God. The latter includes, among other things, the freedom to preach, teach, and write what one interprets to be the word of God to him. Freedom of access to God moves in two directions: it is to God and from God to the individual. This basic freedom should be a prized possession of every child of God.

As one matures he will more consistently exercise or express his essential freedom. One who is mature enough to stand on his own feet may find it necessary at times to say with the early disciples: "We must obey God rather than men." In other words, a mature Christian will not be dominated by others. Furthermore, he will be willing to pay the necessary price to maintain his essential freedom.

It is true that the more mature one is, the more careful he will be how he says a thing, but the more insistent he will also be that he must speak the things that God has spoken to him. There will be times when he must speak if he is to maintain his self-respect as a Christian.

At the same time, to change the pronoun and make it more personal, the more mature we are the more we will respect those who disagree with us. We will recognize and even defend their right to disagree in love. After all, there is at least a bare possibility that we may be wrong.

How desperately the right of dissent needs to be strengthened in some of our churches and denominations, with their agencies and institutions.

The more mature we become, the more willing we will be to limit our freedom regarding nonessentials for the sake of others. True liberty is not freedom to do as we please but freedom to do what we ought. We will not use our freedom "as an opportunity for the flesh," but through love we will use it to serve one another (Gal. 5:13, rsv).

Paul's discussion of the eating of meat offered to idols is a good illustration regarding the proper use of freedom in the area of nonessentials. The mature Christian is free to eat, but because of his love for Christ and the weaker brother he should voluntarily surrender this freedom.

Freedom and maturity interact on one another. One cannot be mature without freedom. On the other hand, the maturer we are, the freer we will be in the area of basic freedom but the more we will respect the freedom of others and the more we will be concerned about the welfare of others. The latter means that increasingly we will be willing to limit our freedom in the area of nonessentials for the sake of others.

The more we mature in our spiritual insight, the more clearly we will see that true freedom for the child of God comes through enslavement to Christ. This is one of the glorious paradoxes of our faith.

Really, the only freedom we have to begin with is the freedom to choose our master: sin and Satan or God and righteousness (see Rom. 6).

# 57. Monologue or Dialogue?

MANY PROBLEMS arise in the area of human relations because of a failure of people to communicate with one another. A major factor contributing to this failure is the inability or the refusal of some people to enter into dialogue.

The latter is one reason for many conflicts that arise between parents and children, teachers and pupils, employers and employees, pastors and people. Also, the clashes between those of different cultures and colors stem to a considerable degree from a failure to carry on real dialogue. Martin Luther King, Jr., in his famous "Letter from the Birmingham Jail," said: "Too long has our beloved Southland been bogged down in a tragic effort to live in monologue rather than dialogue."

The failure to participate in dialogue is primarily but not exclusively the responsibility of the individual or group with the advantage of age, prestige, or power. There is always the possibility of a two-way monologue. Two people or even two groups may seemingly but not really be speaking to one another.

As the younger or less powerful individual or group matures there will be more necessity for dialogue. At least, there will be insistence on an answer to the questions that are asked. Parents of teen-age children become acutely aware of this insistence. But the same thing is true of other individuals and groups. For example, the Negro is now insisting as never before on real dialogue.

The demand by the teen-ager, the college student, the employee, the Negro for dialogue may sound at times like a monologue. If it does, one possible reason is the refusal of the parent, the teacher, the administrator, the white man to enter into dialogue. The more the latter refuses to hear, the louder the former will speak.

Many people prefer monologue to dialogue because dialogue is more difficult. It is usually much easier to state a position than to defend it. Some feel threatened when they are asked to defend

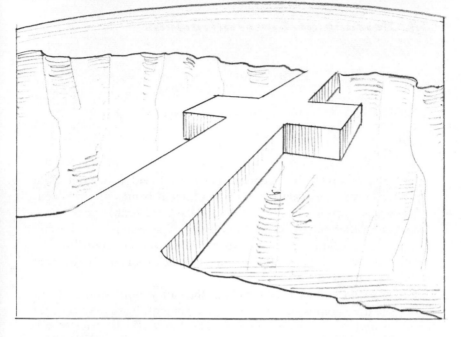

their position. When this happens, usually their reaction will be emotional rather than intelligent.

Also, to carry on effective dialogue one must be able to listen attentively and to analyze objectively the position of the other person or group. This is hard to do. We need to realize, however, that effective communication depends as much on ability to listen as on ability to speak.

Many problems in our churches and denominations stem to a considerable degree from the fact that we tend to speak in monologue rather than dialogue. This is not only true of the preacher in the pulpit but also of the teacher in the classroom and of the denominational leader. There is not enough opportunity for people generally to ask questions, to have a chance to talk back, or to state an opposing viewpoint. Unfortunately, too many of us in church-related vocations are not competent in the use of dialogue.

Dialogue is particularly important in a democracy. There is no real democracy without it. Also, the maturing of people in a democracy will be determined, to a considerable degree, by their participation through dialogue in the life and work of the democracy.

## 58. Beware of Generalizations

THERE ARE relatively few generalizations that will withstand close scrutiny. This is particularly true when human beings are involved.

Many of us are especially prone to make unfavorable generalizations concerning those outside our group. The group may be one of age, class, color, or calling. Such generalizations contribute in significant ways to some of our more serious problems in the area of human relations.

For example, adults may conclude that all young people are in revolt on the campus and in society in general. This may be true of some and even many young people, but it is not true of all. Young people are in the process of becoming adults, of standing on their own feet and making their own decisions. This is a part of the maturing process. But the majority of them are not in revolt.

On the other hand, young people frequently contend that all adults are woefully behind times, that they not only do not understand young people but do not want to understand them. While this may be true of some adults, including some parents, it is not true of all of them. The only accurate generalization that can be made concerning adults is that they are adults. The same is true of young people. And "young" and "adult" are relative terms.

Similar unwise and inaccurate generalizations are frequently made by those belonging to different economic classes. Again, the generalizations are most likely to be unfavorable concerning those belonging to another class. For example, it is just as inaccurate and basically wrong to say that all poor people are lazy and shiftless as it is to say that all rich people are selfish and grasping. The only entirely accurate generalization that can be made is that the poor man is poor and the rich man is rich.

Inaccurate and false generalizations are and have been particularly damaging in the area of race relations. How tragic for any white man to say that "Negroes are inferior." It is equally tragic for any Negro or black man to say that all white people think white people are naturally superior to blacks. The only accurate generalization is to say that the black man is black and the white man is white. Even that generalization can be challenged since there are all shades of color among both blacks and whites.

If we would treat people as individual human beings rather than as members of a particular class or race, it would go a long way toward solving many of the most serious problems of contemporary society.

You will think of other generalizations that are just as inaccurate, unwise, and hurtful as the ones that have been mentioned. Frequently we hear people say: "All preachers are _____"; "Deacons are _____"; "Lawyers are _____"; "Doctors are _____."

If we belong to one of those groups we know that such generalizations are false. Let all of us beware of generalizations, which is another way of saying, "Stop stereotyping."

# 59. God and Natural Phenomena

THE FOLLOWING paragraph appeared in an article in the *Washington Post* concerning the destructiveness of hurricane Camille on the coast of Mississippi and the subsequent floods in Virginia:

> What strikes me as ludicrous is the suggestion . . . that we pray for the survivors. If God has a personal hand in all this (which I do not think) why did he permit such death and terror and horror and heartache in the first place, and if he didn't have anything to do with it, what is the basis for the presumptousness of prayer?

These are old and, to some people, disturbing questions. Many Christians from time to time have asked similar questions.

The questions can be restated somewhat as follows: (1) How is God related to natural phenomena such as hurricanes and floods? (2) Why pray? We will consider primarily the first of these questions and somewhat incidentally the second. As implied in the statement from the *Post* the two questions are very closely related.

Many are disturbed when natural catastrophes occur because they have a distorted conception concerning the relation of God to such catastrophes. It is unfortunate, but much teaching and preaching has led some people to attribute every natural phenomenon to the direct if not miraculous working of the Lord. Many believe that God "sends" the hurricane and the flood.

But these and most other occurrences in the natural order can be explained through the operation of certain basic laws. We know, for example, that there is a "hurricane season," and that there is a general geographic area where most of the hurricanes that hit the United States start or are spawned.

What is true of hurricanes and floods is true of other natural phenomena. Laws may be known or unknown that explain these phenomena, but in the natural order there is a cause for every effect.

It is true that God is the creator of the world and of the laws that govern the world. He sees fit, however, with rare exceptions to let the laws operate or function. This gives us a predictable universe in which to live, and most of us would rather live in such a universe.

Some people may contend that the preceding position makes God "an absentee landlord." This is definitely not true. Notice above the words "with rare exceptions." Man cannot dictate the way God works.

When he wants to, God can step into the process and change the operation of his laws. What he has created he can control. When he does step in in some unusual way, which is a rarity, we can be sure that he has some high and holy purpose in mind. In other words, a lower law may be set aside for a higher law.

There is another sense in which God is not "an absentee landlord." We know by the kind of God revealed in the Scriptures and particularly by the kind of life Jesus lived that God is concerned about people. He reaches out in love to people, particularly people who suffer. This is one reason why we can and should pray for the survivors of a hurricane or a flood and for people in general who suffer regardless of the cause.

The main thrust of our prayers for our own as well as for others should not be that God will build a wall of protection around them that will shield them from the physical and destructive forces of the world. Rather, the burden of our prayers should be that whatever comes with life, the peace that passes understanding and the grace of God that is sufficient may be ours and theirs.

# 60. Committed Critics

MANY ASPECTS of church and denominational life are being reexamined and reevaluated. This reexamination can be healthy. New directions for the work may be established. Creative energies may be released.

The preceding will be true to the degree that the ones who are doing the reexamining are committed to the truth of God and also to the churches as they serve the purposes of God in the world.

It is possible for one to be a critic and not be committed. In that case, his criticism may be valid but his spirit will tend to defeat his purpose. Most of those who are committed will refuse to accept his criticism.

There are critics of some aspects of the work of our churches who are thoroughly committed to the well-being of these churches. Some of those individuals insist that they are critical because they are committed. They contend that if one is genuinely committed to the work of the churches he will be critical of any aspect of that work that needs to be changed, improved, or strengthened.

It will be tragic for our churches and denominations if we refuse to listen to our critics, particularly to those who are committed to the work we are attempting to do.

It is possible that mistakes are being made in the work that will not be corrected because no one calls attention to them. Some people may not speak up because they are afraid of the reactions to what they say.

Some way we must maintain or recover, insofar as it has been lost, the spirit and atmosphere that will make it possible for us to differ and yet to respect and maintain fellowship with one another.

On the other hand, those who see things that need to be corrected should have the courage to speak out. Let such ones be sure, however, that they speak with a sincere desire to help. In other words, it is doubtful if any of us have the right to speak unless we are committed.

TO USE *THIS* INSTRUMENT,
CLASS, YOU MUST FIRST
WRAP IT CAREFULLY
IN LOVE .. AND
WIELD IT WITH A
CAUTIOUS
HUMILITY...

CRITICISM

Also, if and when we feel compelled to speak, let us do it in humility, recognizing that we share some of the responsibility for the conditions we are criticizing. We should never stand aloof from the churches. Rather, we should identify ourselves with them.

If we identify with our church or denomination as we should, we will not be vindictive in what we say. We will never get any personal satisfaction out of criticizing any aspect of the work or any agency. It will be somewhat comparable to criticizing a member of our family.

It should be our desire that our churches and denominations with their institutions and agencies would be better instruments to serve the purposes of God among men. Our prior loyalty to the work of Christ may mean that we must criticize certain phases of the work of our churches and our denominations. But what is best for the kingdom of God ultimately will also be best for the churches.

Criticism from one who is committed to the work of the Lord will always be constructive. It may open wounds, but there will be healing for those wounds in its spirit.